growing up LAKER

growing up LAKER

A Collective Memoir of the First 70 Years

Susan Denise Barnes

Present-day Photos and Contributions
Amy Stewart-Wilmarth

Surrogate Press®

Text Copyright ©2019 Susan Denise Barnes
with contributions by Amy Stewart-Wilmarth

Photos Copyright ©2019 Amy Stewart-Wilmarth

All rights reserved.

No part of this publication may be reproduced, stored in a retrieval system, or transmitted in any form or by any means, electronic, mechanical, photocopying, recording, or otherwise, without written permission of the authors.

Published in the United States by
Surrogate Press®
an imprint of Faceted Press®
Park City, Utah

Surrogate Press, LLC

SurrogatePress.com

ISBN: 978-1-947459-30-4

Library of Congress Control Number: 2019915857

Book cover design by: Michelle Rayner, Cosmic Design LLC

Interior design by: Katie Mullaly, Surrogate Press®

Table of Contents

Preface vii

Acknowledgements xi

INTRODUCTION: Growing Up Laker.......................1

PART I: The Spirit of the Season 5

    CHAPTER ONE: Fall 6

    CHAPTER TWO: Winter....................................37

    CHAPTER THREE: Spring 51

    CHAPTER FOUR: Summer 69

PART II: The Spirit of Place 85

    CHAPTER FIVE: Our Mountains.......................86

    CHAPTER SIX: Our Woods...............................93

    CHAPTER SEVEN: Our Lakes and Beaches 105

    CHAPTER EIGHT: Our Other Dwelling Places......117

PART III: Preserving Our Heritage and Homes 147

PART IV: Growing Up Laker - Final Thoughts 153

About the Authors 156

Notes 158

Bibliography..159

Preface

Long before it became a slogan on t-shirts and coffee mugs the voice in my heart whispered, "the mountains are calling me, and I must go." So, every August we escape the oppressive heat of the emerald Gulf Coast and head to the mountains of North Georgia. We carve out a day or two every so often to hunt for a vacation home. The challenge to the realtor: 1) a large multi-level home surrounded by protected woodlands; 2) a creek or pond on the property or easy access to lakes without motorboats; 3) in or close to a small town. This vision was ensconced in my mind when I opened my email in early 2016.

I received an invitation to a high school class reunion—this one for a newer birthday reunion tradition. The mass invitation stirred the ashes of our collective memories and got the stories burning again. With all that reminiscing going on, an idea for a book kept invading my thoughts—*Growing Up Laker*. Quite frankly I had no real interest in reliving my childhood days in Mountain Lakes or dwelling on their memory; quite the opposite. Possessing average intelligence and little to no athletic, artistic, or social skill, I explored ways to fit in and focused on surviving each day. I looked forward to going to college and never returning. Except for the occasional visit for holidays and to see a few dear friends, nothing lured me back. But then the voice got louder, especially when perusing the Mountain Lakes Facebook pages. Was this email and Facebook chatter and my longing for a home in the woods and mountains mere coincidence? Hmmm. Now I was curious.

Curiosity about what made Mountain Lakes special for kids *Growing Up Laker* was like an itch I couldn't reach. What made the town so unique, so special, that generations of families remained or returned to raise their own children here? What is it that draws hundreds of graduates together every year for reunions to pick up where they left off, whether it's been just one year or 40? And finally, why is it that we can't seem to explain the magic of *Growing Up Laker* to anyone outside of Mountain Lakes? Something about that town, something about those memories. In one sense we have a collective memory; we each walked the same paths, went to the same schools, skated on and swam in the same lakes, roamed the same woods, yet our hearts carry unique memories. Like a kaleidoscope.

Kaleidoscope: n. 1. A tube shaped optical instrument that is rotated to produce a succession of symmetrical designs by means of mirrors reflecting the constantly changing patterns made by bits of colored glass at one end of the tube. 2. A series of changing phases or events.

Preface

A kaleidoscope is a cylindrical tube with three mirrors inside in a triangular configuration. There is an eyehole at one end and a collection of objects at the other end of the tube. Although the container holding the objects is as large as the kaleidoscope tube, only the objects within the space of the triangle are reflected. The images you see when you look through the eyehole will never be repeated; they are unique and fleeting, but the magic lingers. And, so it is with the kaleidoscope of *Growing Up Laker* memories. Our collective memory of events, places, and experiences belong to everyone, yet there are a few special ones that remain uniquely ours. That is the magic of *Growing Up Laker*.

Acknowledgements

Thanks to all who took part in this stroll down memory lane. First to our fathers, James Lee Barnes (Class of 1951) and Thomas Raymond Stewart (Class of 1943), who treasured growing up Laker and raised their own families here. Their stories, diaries, and photographs lent special meaning to this project. We also thank our mothers, Clara Sue Barnes and Nancy Elliot Stewart who taught us valuable lessons, dusted us off when we stumbled, and sparked and supported our passions and pursuits.

Second, we extend a hearty thanks to the Mountain Lakes Historic Preservation Committee (HPC) members and their vision of preserving Mountain Lakes history through the eyes of its residents. We are indebted to those who spearheaded the oral history (Laker Profiles) and historical essay projects. May they continue to flourish.

Third, we are grateful to Amy's brother Tom Stewart ('72) who provided a beautiful illustration of my grandparent's home at 105 Kenilworth Road to include in our book. The drawing is based on a 1937 family photo. I am indebted to him for capturing this treasured family photo.

Finally, thanks to all the kids who experienced *Growing Up Laker*—the first kids sharing their stories through the HPC Laker Profiles, the 156 participants in the Growing Up Laker Survey conducted August 2016, and our Facebook Friends (You know you're from Mountain Lakes if…)—whose memories fueled our journey.

Growing Up Laker

Introduction

Patricia Reid Herold's book *Mountain Lakes 1911-2011*, commissioned by the Borough of Mountain Lakes Historic Preservation Committee, depicts 100 years of life in Mountain Lakes. As a resident or former resident, it's a wonderful read. Not only does it delight the reader with the history of Mountain Lakes, it provides insight into the origins of the Spirit of Mountain Lakes. This centennial celebration book and a curiosity about why people rave about growing up in Mountain Lakes form the catalyst for our book, *Growing Up Laker: A Collective Memoir of the First 70 Years*.

Small town living conjures up a list of descriptors, positive or negative depending on your perspective. On one hand, small town living means everyone knows everyone else. Small towns embody a spirit of community and caring. There is a sense of similarity and shared values. Small towns provide a sense of freedom—freedom to explore, to play, to experience the world around us. Small towns shelter residents from city living—the chaos, the crime, the traffic. They offer the opportunity to commune with nature and lead a slower, simpler life. Small towns are easy to navigate and traverse. On the other hand, they may lack shopping and entertainment options. Small towns may have limited work opportunities. They often create a narrow perspective of the world because of their homogenous makeup. But if you grew up in Mountain Lakes, you realize we had all the benefits of small-town life and access to a great big world right outside our door.

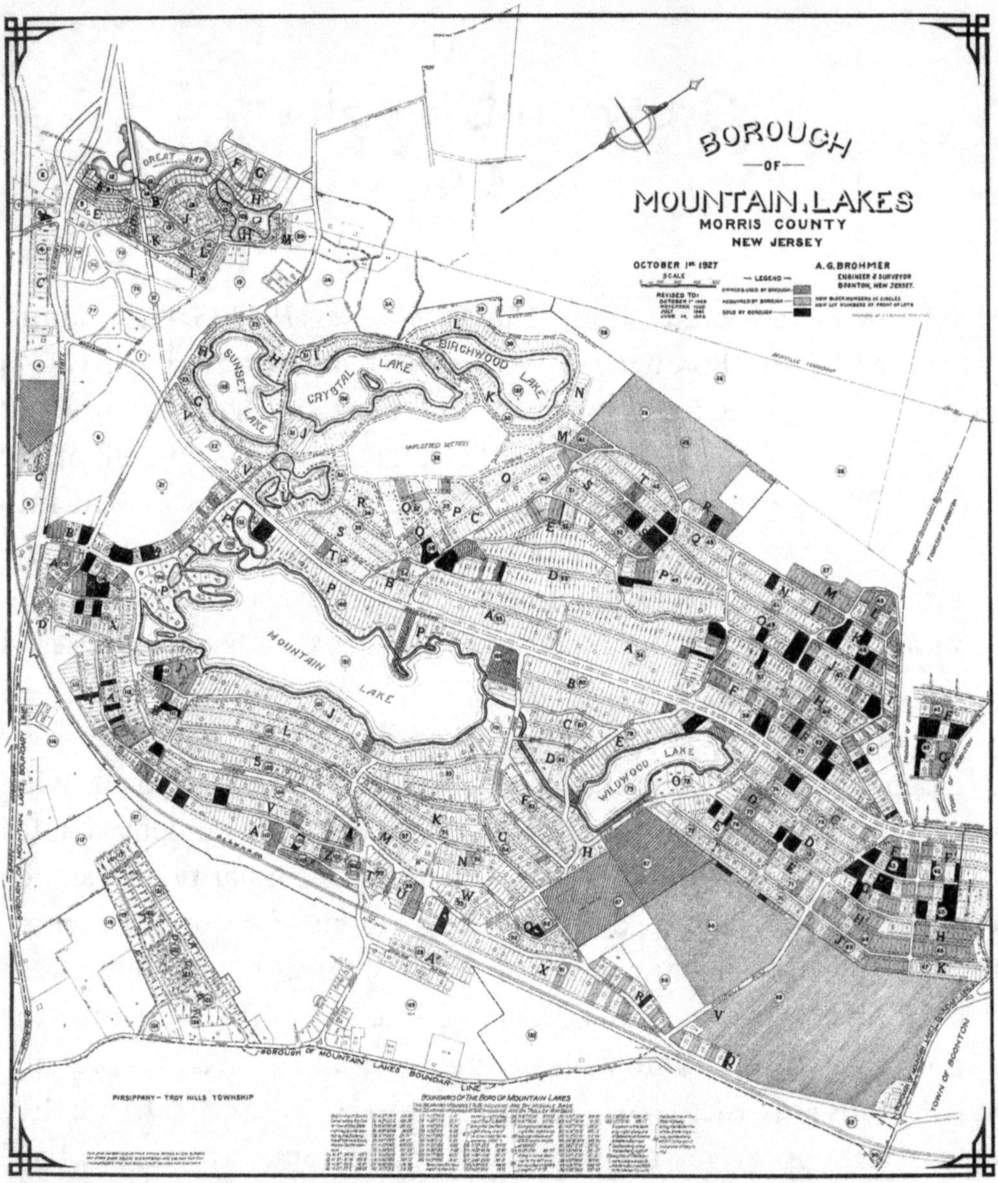

1927 Map of Mountain Lakes.

Creating the Town

Fueled by a desire to create an ideal and unique community, Herbert Hapgood set out to find the perfect location. Lewis Van Duyne knew just the place by combining several owners' properties into a single parcel of land for development. In 1908 Herbert Hapgood and Lewis Van Duyne stood atop a ridge, looked across an expanse of undeveloped wilderness, and sealed the deal—1,000 acres of land which would become Mountain Lakes Residential Park (Herold 2010).

Hapgood's vision was to create a residential park that would eclipse the character and amenities of other similar residential parks in northern New Jersey and New York. Not only would residents have access to New York City, they would be surrounded by the lush natural environs that northern New Jersey had to offer. He wanted his residents to be of a "particular character" as well, marketing Mountain Lakes as place for "high class, refined people." From part-time bungalows to permanent luxurious estates, Hapgood offered it all. When Hapgood's empire collapsed, the Belhall Construction Company moved in to

Pillars mark the entrance to the town.

complete Hapgood's projects and fill other vacant lots with its style of homes (Herold 2010). The early architects and builders created the infrastructure and the one-of-a-kind natural beauty of Mountain Lakes, but it was the early residents that created the community and ignited the Laker Spirit.

Creating the Laker Spirit

The first residents of Mountain Lakes arrived in 1911: The Luellens, Wellers, Garnaus, Backers, Houstons, Sweets, Lows, and Clevelands, to name a few. After a few parties, they wasted little time establishing the Mountain Lakes Association. The association served a dual purpose; to foster beneficial relations with Hapgood's company as he developed Mountain Lakes, and to create a foundation for the management of the community and its residents. The constitution and by-laws served to organize the community, encourage mutual respect, and preserve the spirit of Mountain Lakes which endures to this day (Herold 2010). But what comprises the Spirit of Mountain Lakes beyond these first by-laws and constitutions? Hmmm. The importance of education and appreciation for cultural experiences; a sense of community; freedom to explore, enjoy, and protect our natural resources; and perhaps most importantly, an indefinable Laker bond that lasts a lifetime.

We travel through the seasons celebrating iconic Laker events, explore popular hangouts, and revisit Mountain Lakes landmarks to unravel the mystery and spirit of *Growing Up Laker*. We gathered stories from an online survey conducted in 2016 and gleaned stories from the Mountain Lakes Historic Preservation Committee's Laker Profiles and historical essays. Finally, we posed questions on Mountain Lakes Facebook sites and retrieved some of those fond memories. These memories span seven decades—from Mountain Lakes' beginnings to early 1980s. We invite you to join our reminiscence. We hope you enjoy this kaleidoscope of memories and will be inspired to do some of your own storytelling. Through it all we strive to honor our Laker Spirit.

Part 1

The Spirit of the Season

Every living system—human, flora, fauna—has a unique cycle it follows and so it was with the Mountain Lakes community. For kids *Growing Up Laker,* the cycle began with the new school year, ran through the seasons, and started anew on Labor Day Weekend. The rhythm and routine of this Laker cycle lent a sense of structure, security, certainty, and anticipation to our lives as kids. We reveled in the kaleidoscope of changing seasons and welcomed the magic and excitement that our Laker traditions promised.

In this chapter, we invite you to walk, or ride, with us through the seasons—the events and traditions that seem uniquely Laker.

Fall
Chapter One

Wildwood Lake.

The dragonflies are thick as I sit in the neighbor's rowboat on Shadow Lake. They always seem to take over the sky in late August. It's quieter now…swim season and the culminating championship meets are over. Families are on late summer vacations, typically to other places with lots of water, which always seemed funny to me considering all the lakes we have in our own little town. Labor Day swim races at the Mountain Lakes Club are the final races of the season and mean nothing more than another opportunity to compete and hang out with friends.

Back to School

Moms are flipping through the Sears and Montgomery Ward catalogs while others are dragging their kids to Main Street in Boonton for Buster Brown shoes and PF Flyer sneakers, and to neighboring towns for back to school shopping. Our parents travel for miles to buy clothes—to New York City (Macy's, Sax Fifth Avenue, Wannamaker's, Best & Company), Morristown (Bamberger's, Epsteins), Rockaway, Paramus, Short Hills, and Willowbrook Malls, the Laurie Shop, Peg Merrick Shop, Tweed's Children's Clothing Store, Two Guys from Harrison, and many more long forgotten. And of course, we head over to Williams Stationery and the 5 & 10 Stores at Del's Village for school supplies—the canvas blue notebooks, the zippered pen and pencil holders that hooked onto the rings of the notebook, a package of Bic pens, a package of orange #2 pencils, a ruler, lined note paper, and subject dividers. Afterward, we head to Marcello Brothers for our gym uniforms and other sports stuff. Whether you were a family with two kids or twelve, it was both a ritual and an adventure getting ready for the new school year.

For most the new year starts January 1st, but for kids *Growing Up Laker*, the new year starts with Labor Day weekend. This three-day portal marks the end of everything good about summer and the sweet hope for a great new school year. As Jack Maypole ('85) notes, we had a love-hate relationship with Labor Day weekend and back to school. *"Things were winding up, the freedom…of the warm season was soon to be replaced by wearing scratchy new clothes…For the most part, I think some of us just weren't ready to stop being barefoot and carefree and riding bikes till the streetlights came on."*[4]

We recall the newness of the year: hot and scratchy new school clothes (summer's still with us); the smell of new supplies (the pencils, erasers, plastic zip cases to keep them in); lockers (and locker combinations!); gym uniforms; and making book covers out of paper bags. We anticipate the new school year with a *"sense that this year might be better."*[3] We hope the trials of last year are past us and anxiously await new experiences, somewhat secure in the rhythm of *Growing Up Laker* daily school routines.

Back to School List

- Big notebook—3 ring binder Blue fabric one or one that says Mountain Lakes
- Notebook dividers
- Notebook paper—please get the narrow lines!
- Book covers (Mom, can we get real ones instead of using paper bags?)
- #2 Pencils and pencil sharpener and extra erasers (flat pink or rectangular green)
- Bic pens—blue and black
- Ruler
- Compass
- Zipper pouch for pens/pencils to hook in notebook
- Book strap so I don't lose my books when I ride my bike
- New gym uniform, sneakers and gym socks
- Gym bag and sports stuff
- New shoes, clothes, fall jacket

Back to school also meant back to walking with purpose—getting to school on time instead of aimlessly wandering the town as we did all summer. Walking to school was standard practice for kids *Growing Up Laker,* but for new kids just in from the concrete jungles of the city, it was a whole new experience.

It was a huge change from growing up in Union City and Jersey City. The population in Union City was 65,000 at the time, in a space smaller than Mtn. Lakes, we lived in a house with three apartments. If I had stayed in the city, it would have required two buses to get to school. The move to Mtn. Lakes was traumatic. The town was unreal, a fairy tale environment. I had never seen so many trees and lakes and streams.

My fondest memories of the fall were walking to high school from our home on Wildwood Lake through the football field and down the path from Briarcliff to the back of the high school. The mornings were chilly as the leaves began to change colors, we would cross the football field and enter what seemed to me to be a forest and emerge five minutes later at the high school (Richard Lotti, '74).[3]

We arrived by foot, by bike, or maybe by a kind parent on a raining-cats-n-dogs day to those massive stone schools that seemed ancient. Well, they were in a way, but those buildings didn't magically appear. A great deal of creativity, debate, and money was expended to ensure the educational needs of the growing kid population were met. Let's take a quick look at the building of our Mountain Lakes schools.

A Bit of School History

Early founding families recognized the joys and importance of outdoor living, cultural engagement and activities, and community celebrations and gatherings. They also were cognizant of the importance of education. Schools were not part of Hapgood's marketing strategy; however, they were an essential element to the earliest residents. To this day, education remains a Laker priority. Patricia Reid Herold's book, *Mountain Lakes, 1911-2011,* gives a thorough account of the history of Mountain Lakes school system and the building of its schools. We provide a glimpse to signify the importance of education to Mountain Lakes residents and how tough it was to keep up with a growing community.

The first residents were settling into town during the Progressive movement in America, both politically and educationally. In 1912, a progressive President Woodrow Wilson defeats two other candidates who also consider themselves progressives. According to John Steen, Borough Historian (1993-1997), educational efforts in the early Laker years were heavily influenced by both the new political pulse and the progressive educational movement inspired by the works of John Dewey.

Shortly after the first residents arrived, classes were set up in a small house at 8 Larchdell Way funded by Hanover Township and Mountain Lakes residents. Classes were held in two converted bedrooms (the teachers lived rent free in the rest of the house) and The School of Individual Instruction followed the methods of Ella Frances Lynch, a disciple of John Dewey's educational philosophy. Ruth Doremus (b. 1898, arrived in ML 1911) recalls *"There were 11 of us in the school starting with Kindergarten and going up to the sixth grade. When you got through the sixth grade you had to go to Boonton for school."*[1]

Even in its first year, the school proved too small to handle the number of kids. Hanover Township agreed to rent a larger building and Hapgood offered space in business buildings near the railroad station on Midvale Road for the school (Yaccarinos, Mountain Lakes Market, etc.). School operations moved in 1913 to the store buildings, but once again, the classrooms filled up faster than the chalk dust could settle.

Lake Drive School

It was time for a proper school—a new school—so the Mountain Lakes School House (aka the Old Stone School) was built on Lake Drive between the Boulevard and the Mountain Lakes Club. The two-acre lot was donated, and Hanover Township paid $23,000 for its construction. While some accounts attribute the donation of the property to Hapgood, Myrtle Hillman Kingsley (b. 1915) recalled the *"Friesleben's had given that property for a school. They lived right across the street there… it's sort of a silly place for a school, right smack on the water."*[1] The school marked its official opening on 14 November 1914.

> *The Lake Drive School…was the first school building to be erected in the community. It is situated on the corner of Lake Drive and the*

Boulevard next to the Mountain Lakes Club and occupies an ideal lakefront setting. Built for elementary grades, it has ten classrooms, an art room, a gymnasium, and an auditorium with a seating capacity of three-hundred (Correll and Koster, *Picturesque Mountain Lakes* 1958, 24).

Despite the new building and an expansion six years later to house K-9th grade, the school just couldn't keep pace with the influx of new families and kids. Ralph Osgood Wells (b. 1916) remembers *"When I was in fifth grade, they couldn't take care of them all, so we had a split session. Half of us went one month in the morning, other half went in the afternoon."*[1] John N. Brown (b. 1920) recalls heading back to the original Larchdell Way Schoolhouse when classrooms got crowded. *"I started school in the first grade in the Stone School at age five"* and *"by third grade we were in the Larchdell Way house…continued through ninth grade."*[1]

For the next 20 years, students graduated from the Mountain Lakes School House and went out of town—Boonton, Morristown, etc.—for 10th-12th grade. Eventually the desire for a high school of our own prompted action. We were in the midst of the Great Depression, many homes were empty, and folks were seeking expansion at a time when New Deal programs were offering government funds to erect public buildings and put people to work.

Briarcliff School

Briarcliff School was built despite fervent opposition to the use of funding from the Public Works Administration established by President Roosevelt. Many residents lauded the opportunity to grow the community; others lamented that these government programs would bankrupt the nation. It took three referendums to secure funding, but when it was all said and done, Mountain Lakes could finally boast of an educational system that carried students from kindergarten to high school graduation in a modern new facility. *"It was the utmost in modern functional design having nine classrooms, two science laboratories, a home economics laboratory, a library, a manual training shop, a cafeteria, locker and shower rooms, an art room and an auditorium-gymnasium with a stage"* (Correll and Koster 1958, 25). Mountain Lakes held its first high school graduation in 17 June 1938.

Wildwood School

Approved for construction in 1951, 4.7 acres were allocated to build a new school on Glen Road. Named Wildwood School for its proximity to Wildwood Field, it was built specifically for K-2nd grade and opened its doors in 1953. Yet again the community grew and on 27 March 1966 a new modern addition was dedicated. In keeping with the progressive educational philosophy, the design placed the classrooms around the library like a donut. Teachers could open the walls between the classrooms for shared learning experiences.

For half the year while the addition was being built, 4th grade students found themselves displaced, some of us among giants at the high school. At times we had the misfortune of being in the hallway when classes were changing or choking from the cigarette smoke in the restrooms. When the time came to move back to Wildwood, we marched with our bag of books and supplies up the Path and across the football field to our new classrooms. Imagine that happening today!

Photo courtesy of MLHS.

Mountain Lakes High School—Powerville Road

Mountain Lakes ran out of room for grade school kids at Lake Drive prompting the building of Wildwood in 1951 and now Briarcliff Junior/High School was following suit. After a much heated debate (remember the Briarcliff battle?) over expansion vs a new building, construction of a new brick high school on Powerville Road was approved.

> *The new High School will contain a spacious cafeteria, a well-equipped library, three new science laboratories with the latest equipment, and a regulation sized gymnasium with bleachers and a folding door which divides the gym into two smaller physical education areas. In the future an auditorium will be added....In order to take full advantage of the new facilities, the Board of Education is making important changes in the present curriculum which will raise the educational standards of Mountain Lakes to an even higher level.* (Correll and Koster 1958, 26)

The expansion Correll and Koster speak of happened in the early 1970s. We recall watching the construction through classroom windows.

Growing Up Laker

The new high school celebrated its first graduating class in 1959. In the 1962 high school yearbook, it's noted that this class held a dual distinction: the 25th graduating high school class in Mountain Lakes and the first class to complete four years in the Powerville Road High School.

Every student in the Class of '62 is well acquainted with both Briarcliff and Powerville School. Twenty-five classes have been graduated from these two schools, the Class of '62 being the Silver Class; but this title is not our only honor. The Class of '62 is also the first class to complete four years at the "new" Mountain Lakes High School. Our class has seen this building changed from a meaningless structure to THE High School, full of life, atmosphere, and spirit. (1962 MLHS Yearbook, 4)

Over the years, kids *Growing Up Laker* were bounced around as town officials and educators puzzled over where to squeeze us all in. We anxiously awaited the arrival of our final report card to discover next year's school destination.

"Learning my 4th grade fate!"

Nursery Schools

Lots of kids *Growing Up Laker* began their educational careers in nursery school. Was the abundance of nursery schools in the 1950s through the 1970s a result of parents' emphasis on education, an economic necessity, or just an opportunity to give mothers a break? Whatever the reason, nursery schools sprang up on every corner. Laurel Hill and Condit Road held the three most remembered: Mrs. Haydock's, Mrs. Cody/Mrs. Mills, and Mrs. Hartmann's.

The Harriet Field Nursery School, named for Mrs. Haydock's mother and later known simply as Mrs. Haydock's, opened in 1954 and offered morning sessions for three- and four-year-olds (*This is Mountain Lakes*, 1979). At Mrs. Haydock's, there were monkey and bunny hooks to hang up our coats on the left wall as you entered the front door. The weight of the coats made the monkeys smile (Bonnie Bedford Parks, John Mills).[4] Liz Merrit also remembers *"a tree swing…[with] a seat in the shape of a pumpkin…live guinea pigs, hamsters and rabbits….And most memorable of all, the secret door between the coat closet…and the kitchen."*[4]

The Hartmann Nursery-Kindergarten school opened in 1960 on Condit Road. The school offered morning and afternoon sessions. Ninety to 100 children attended nursery and kindergarten here annually. The school also offered individualized educational programs to match the children's developmental needs and interests (*This is Mountain Lakes*, 1979).

Mrs. Polly Cody owned and operated a nursery school called the Mountain Lakes Cooperative Nursery School. Peter Mills ('74) notes *"I went to Mrs. Cody's nursery school. My mom was an assistant. The next year the Cody's moved to Illinois and my mom bought (or inherited) the school. She ran the school out of our house which was across the street from Haydock's."*[4]

Although the nursery schools on the hill seem best remembered, other children recall going to the Community Church and to Mrs. Prahl's in Boonton in the late 1940s and 1950s. In 1975, the Lakeland

Growing Up Laker

Mountain Lakes Cooperative Nursery School.

YMCA offered a small nursery program called Kaleidoscope. And then there were the kids like me who just went to kindergarten at St. John's instead. Wherever you started out, it led you to a common Laker school.

St. John's School

St. John's School, later known as The Wilson School (and now The Craig School), is located on the corner of the Boulevard and Tower Hill Road. This private Episcopal school was founded by the Reverend Henry B. Wilson in 1909 and named for the sponsoring church, St. John's in Boonton. The school provided a quality education with a focus on preparing students for college. Students from surrounding towns attended kindergarten through 12th grade for girls; K-8, for boys. David Higgins (b. 1922) shared his memory:

> *I went to St. John's School, which is now The Wilson School. It was a private school for boys through the eighth grade. Girls went up through high school. At that time, you went to either Boonton High*

School or Morristown High School. I went to Montclair Academy. I used to commute to Montclair on old public service bus route 116. It took about an hour. I guess my folks thought I'd get a better education than what they knew of Boonton and Morristown schools.[1]

For the longest time, there was no age requirement to attend kindergarten at St. John's, so many parents sent their kids at an early age, then transferred them to the public school. And although most of us graduated from Mountain Lakes High School, we were denied the "attended K-12" distinction in the graduation program because we went to St. John's.

Top: St. John's Spring Program 1960 (Future Class of 1972).
Bottom: St. John's Thanksgiving Program 1961 (Future Class of 1974).

Since the first days of Mountain Lakes Residential Park, education has been the number one priority for its residents. Soon the quality of education afforded to its citizens rivaled nature's bounty as the main attraction for parents desiring a better life for their kids. As word spread, the town was hard pressed to keep pace with the burgeoning student population. Through all the additions and changes however, some experiences remained universal for kids *Growing Up Laker* the first 70 years.

Some Things Never Change

There are as many school memories as there are students who passed through the doors of each Mountain Lakes school. Stories of traveling to and from school, events, and antics seem to transcend time. Some of our favorites—spanning 70 years—are here. We hope they inspire you to recount a few memories of your own.

School Transportation... Walk!

There was only one way to get to and from school. Except for a few lucky folks who lived far enough away to ride the trolley/bus, we walked to school in the morning, home in the afternoon, and did the same at lunch time. Those who didn't live quite far enough away to catch the bus or trolley were often the most vocal of the lamenters. Complaining yielded no results. Neither snow nor rain nor heat will keep Laker kids from walking to school!

Myrtle Hillman Kingsley (b. 1915) remembers

My brother...and I went to first grade together. We were very jealous because the kids that came from Dixon's Coal Yard got free trolley tickets because they lived a certain [distance] from the school. You could go to the school and buy 50 cents worth of tickets...Then on really stormy days we were allowed to take the trolley.[1]

Once the trolley system ended, kids were on their own again. George Wilson ('45) calls to mind:

Fall

I used to walk to school every morning from over there at the coal yard, right over Lake Drive, 3.3 miles to the Lake Drive School. School was never postponed because of inclement weather, because there weren't any buses running.... I don't care how long it rained, you walked to school. They just said, "Oh, you walk to school," and the teachers would put your clothes on the radiator and let them dry out.[1]

Walking from Intervale Road, Tom Brackin ('53) used to cut across Neafie's Field, even as a kindergartener.

Well, it was a rolling field which was absolutely wonderful for playing. Kids loved it because the grass grew about as high as your nose and you could run through all these paths. There were trees on the borderlines...It was the only way you could get from Intervale Road and Yorke Village. You had to cross through that and then you were up by the [Railroad] Station, and on to school.... One morning I got up to the edge of the field and there was so much fog I couldn't see across the field. I was alone. I turned around and walked back to the house. My grandmother who lived there, too, said: "What are you doing back here?" So, my mother and she drove me to school that day. But it was a walk to and from every day."[1]

Shocking? No. Most of us have a tale or two of getting lost or distracted on our way to school as five- and six-year-olds! I certainly do. It was just a part of *Growing Up Laker.*

As much as we liked to fuss about having to walk to and from school, it wasn't all that bad. It was a community activity, a common denominator, a fact of life. The kid who lived farthest away would set the wheels in motion. At every house or intersection another kid or two would join the march. Pretty soon there'd be eight or more of us walking along. Our morning walk to school started at Crane Road, along the Boulevard past Overlook, Laurel Hill, down Lake Drive and Dartmouth, and ended at Briarcliff for junior high school or continued down the Path to the high school.

The Boulevard sidewalk follows the original trolley line and runs from North Pocono Road to Fanny Road.

We'd laugh, solve the pressing teen problem of the week, and sing ridiculous songs…"The ants go marching one by one hurrah, hurrah…" At times we'd mix it up by walking all the way down the Boulevard to Beechway and then to the high school. Naturally, we picked up a few more friends along that route.

"*By the time you got halfway to school, there were twenty kids walking along! And you flirted, you joked, you fooled around, you threw rocks at squirrels running down the wire. It was fun*" (George Wilson, '45).[1] Graduating 15 years later, Lynn Honicky Jones ('60) recalls "*walking to/from school with neighborhood kids was the best…we had a defined route and would pick up friends along the way…solved all of the world's problems each and every day on this journey!*"[3] And 31 years later, Lorraine Lotti Wagner ('76) echoes that same sentiment "*As a High School student, of course I spent time along the path from Briarcliff to the High School. That lovely path and the stream became our home during those years. It's where we talked about life, dreamed about the future and dealt with our teenage problems together.*"[3]

Lunchtime

Walking to and from school was one thing but going home for lunch... well, that's hard for outsiders and younger generations to comprehend. Yes, not only did we walk to and from school each day, we walked to and from school at lunch time. Some of the neighborhood mothers formed carpools to transport kids at lunchtime. Thank goodness! Now we lollygaggers and slow-pokes actually had time to eat something!

Although standard practice was for kids to go home at lunchtime, there were occasions when kids stayed for lunch. For those few, there were accommodations. Kids brought their lunch and ate in the gym or another makeshift lunchroom. There was another alternative, however—lunch at the Mountain Lakes Club!

For decades, kids slipped through the hedges and up the back stairs of the Club to get lunch. Constance Witham Higgins (b. 1919) recalls the school *"was right next to the Club, so we could go next door and go up the steps to their kitchen and buy an ice cream cone for five cents."*[1] Faith Witham Robertson (Constance's sister) adds, *"We'd go up the outside stairs and put our order in, to have a hamburger; the only item on the menu. We couldn't eat at the Club....We'd go back to the school and eat in the gym, which was used as a lunchroom; no tables or chairs — we sat on the concrete steps."*[1] In the 1960s kids remember eating lunch Tuesdays-Fridays in a little dining area next to the kitchen.

Social and Recreational Events

Once school was over, it was on to fun! We had lots of options: hacking around on the school yard, invading the nearest friend's home for snacks and play, or waiting around for the Good Humor truck if we had allowance in our pockets. When we got older, there were sports practices, school clubs, and other local hangouts that kept us occupied. Our schools weren't just places of learning, they also provided athletic, social, and recreational events. Along with the usual school dances, there were canteens and summer recreation (more on that later). From the adults' perspective, the Canteen program provided an acceptable and safe social outlet for junior and senior high school teens. In other words, it kept us off the streets and out of trouble. Kids could play sports in the gym, dance to live music by local bands in the lunchroom or just hang out and play cards and board games. For some, Canteen was an excuse to get out of the house and into some mischief of their own.

A Gum-Chewer's Victory

Gum-chewing was verboten in the hallowed halls of learning; however, *nothing* could dissuade a girl from her favorite pastime. Writing "I will not chew gum in class" 100 times in third grade did not curtail it. Sticking it on her nose as punishment in sixth grade only strengthened her defiance. Typing class detention had no effect (speedy typing would never be her forte!). The proof lies in the 132-foot gum wrapper chain hanging on the wall.

Football

Nothing says Laker Spirit like sports, and in the fall football reigned supreme. Yes, we had cross country, soccer, and field hockey...but let's face it....they didn't compare with football frenzy. High school football was a sporting event, a music event, a social event, and even an excuse to get out of doing yard work. If we lived close enough to the football field, the sound of the band practicing before the game was our rallying cry. We sat, stood, meandered, watched, listened, and noshed during heat, rain, wind, and snow as the HERD (and marching band) worked its magic on the gridiron. We leave it to the players, statisticians, sports historians and other devoted fans to fill you in on facts and specific events. Suffice it to say, there was only one place to be on a Saturday afternoon in the fall in Mountain Lakes. So, while you wait for the stories to flow, we'll fill you up with some early football trivia and the building of Wildwood Field.

One of the earliest stories we have is from Frank Wiswall who was born in 1919 and grew up in Mountain Lakes. Back then, our schools only went to 8th grade; so, Frank went to Boonton and graduated in 1937.

Sport wise, yes there was [a rivalry between Mountain Lakes and Boonton]. It was written up in the papers. They said that Boonton had never beaten Mountain Lakes in football. That got my hair up because my junior year and my senior year I was on the second team, played left guard for Boonton. The powers that be, the coaches or whatever, one time managed to make a game between Boonton's second team and Mountain Lakes' first team. I loved that because I knew everybody on the first team. What the heck, I grew up with them. We beat them. Boonton did beat Mountain Lakes in football. Some things you don't forget.[1]

Mountain Lakes formed its first football team in 1936, launching a tradition that stands first in line even today. During those early days of football, towns everywhere did their best to create playing fields. High schools even travelled to other towns to play their games when they didn't have fields of their own. Carolyn Carlson Mills ('43) notes *"Fall was football which was a bit of a problem in that we did not have a home field but played on a field in Denville which meant a ride of some kind.... If we won a football game (that was a major event) we would have a "snake dance" thru town and a bonfire at Island Beach."*[1]

High school football field pressbox dedicated to Skip Watts, long-time resident and "Voice of the Herd."

Skip Watts ('44) and Carolyn Carlson Mills share the tale of the 1942 championship game against Netcong High School. Netcong High School only had an 80-yard football field. *"After a run for a touchdown you were then moved back to the 20 yard line to try again"* (Carolyn Carlson Mills).[1] *"Russ Granton was fullback and Russ cut through the line, ran all the way through the end zone, jumped the fence and ran into a cemetery that was there, which was the reason why the field was only 80 yards"* (Skip Watts).[1]

It was time for Mountain Lakes to have a field of its own, so they built it...from the ground up you might say. It was a combined effort—gym class, American Legion, and others. Skip Watts and David Higgins tell the story.

Gym class in high school consisted of going down and cutting down trees and clearing the brush to make what's now Wildwood Field. It was a rather primitive facility. You may remember too that the American Legion, who was very active in Mountain Lakes at that time, were really the people who pressed for that field led by Paul Dillon and that crew, and Rip Schultz and that gang who were in the American Legion. They were the ones who pushed to have that field built (Skip Watts).[1]

David Higgins (b. 1922) provides more detail:

The American Legion Post—my dad was the post commander—undertook the job of cutting the trees out. All by axe and hand saw. Trees about six, eight inches in diameter. The legionnaires, their sons [cut down the trees]. I was one of them. It started in the fall and most of the winter, and on into the spring. Oaks, maples, I suppose some sycamores. The chestnuts were gone. There were no evergreens, just hardwoods. [The fallen trees] were the big problem. We had a hell of a job cleaning them up. We couldn't give the firewood away. One Saturday, a couple fellas and myself got down there, early in the morning, before the men got down there. We decided to burn some of it. Got away from us. So, we had to call Freddy Webb at the firehouse to come down with some Indian tanks and put it out. He says, next time you want to do this, get some brooms and some Indian tanks.[1]

Fast forward a few decades and the Mountain Lakes football program gives rise to the HERD ethos in 1967 and an unquenchable desire for victory on the field. Chris Jenny ('73) notes:

Football and fall sports? The birth of the HERD in the late '60s. I was in Briarcliff at the time, but who can forget the big game against Glen Ridge in 1967 that was the turning point of the program. They had owned us forever, and Bobby Wilson and company went out and thrashed them 37-13. It was like a dream come true for us kids! And the rest, as they say, is history.[3]

The boys' sports program was more than teaching kids how to be athletes. It taught the guys valuable lessons: responsibility, dedication, hard work, teamwork, loyalty. It was a fraternity—a brotherhood that lasted a lifetime.

We felt we needed a concept of success that any kid interested in football could accomplish. We wanted something unique, thus the concept of the H.E.R.D. built on the principles of Hustle, Enthusiasm, Roughness, and Desire. - Coach Doug Wilkins

Entrance to Wildwood Field (top).
Dedication plaque for Coach Doug Wilkins (bottom).

Football wasn't the only excitement on the field. Cheerleaders in crisp uniforms and polished saddle shoes lined the track in front of the stands coaxing the crowd to chant "Here we go Lakers, here we go!" and "Hold that line!" The marching band with twirlers and color guard worked their magic at halftime. Like the players and spectators, they were there come rain or shine...at times losing a shoe or boot on the muddy field. Half-time also provided a backdrop for other memorable events. Do you remember the Miss Mountain Lakes Ugly Pageant? It stirred up the town like nothing we'd ever experienced. It was fall of 1972—a time of student protests around the nation. Doug McWilliams ('71) tells us the story.

> *My sister Lisa instituted this thing called the Miss Mountain Lakes Ugly Pageant. It was an anti-homecoming thing.... They had people with old beat up convertibles that would take these girls around dressed in various strange ways. My sister hooked up with somebody...and put together a little show...It was...halftime...The guy and my sister Lisa got out of the car as it came around the track, ran out to the middle of the field and unfurled the peace flag, which was a red and white striped flag with a peace symbol. At a quick glance, of course, it looked somewhat like an American flag. They stuck it in the ground and lit it on fire. The stands, particularly the visiting stands, emptied onto the field and a riot took place. It was total bedlam.[1]*

Growing Up Laker

As we looked out across the playing field, over the opponents' bleachers, we beheld the iconic fall sights that rivaled our love of football. The magnificence of a Laker fall was captivating, resulting in an appreciation for nature's beauty eternally branded in our Laker hearts and spirit.

More Fall Fun

Fall in full bloom equated to the family tradition of raking the leaves and disposing of them. We spent hours battling the wind while raking the leaves. It only took one gust to wipe out an afternoon's work. We raked a small portion of leaves to the street to burn and the rest of the leaves we raked into jumping piles. When we were done having fun, we loaded them into Dad's orange and white silk parachute and hauled them off to the woods on the side of the house.

Steve McCurdy ('72) notes:

We were still allowed to have open fires and every year in the fall after inviting the neighborhood kids to help us rake our lawn, my parents would have a giant bon-fire on the beach next to the lake and cook hot dogs and marshmallows. The neighbor parents were always

Fall

a bit resentful that their kids were helping us rake our leaves but not volunteering to do so at home![3]

Tom Stewart ('72) recalls *"the smell of burning leaves in the air every weekend and hauling our leaves into the backyard woods with old bedspreads to carry/drag them."*[3] His list of memories also includes:

- *ALWAYS having plenty of apples in the pantry and I have never found apples that have tasted as good as those since*
- *Tackle football in the front yards of the neighborhood. A few bloody noses but no broken bones. Maybe a concussion or two…*
- *Collecting thousands of acorns in paper grocery bags, hiding them in secret places in the woods, using them as ammo for weekend acorn fights* [3]

Acorns, water, eggs, and other artillery were great defenses, especially when Mischief Night rolled around.

Mischief Night

Again, some things never change when we're *Growing Up Laker*, and that includes the tradition of Mischief Night. Once a year mischief reigns—innocence unleashed in a frenzy of shaving cream, toilet paper, eggs, and cherry bombs. Town police turn their heads…to an extent. Two of the most famous stories involve a chicken and a church bell. While we aren't sure these are truly Mischief Night pranks, they certainly exemplify the type of antics we pulled. Skip Watts admits being the architect of both pranks.

The Mueser's, who lived on Lake Drive, kept chickens. So, we [Skip and cousin, Harvey] proceeded to swipe a chicken from the Muesers, take it around [to the Club]. We opened the door and threw the chicken in the lobby and slammed it. Mr. Shuer, who had a bit of a shaking problem anyhow, practically went crazy with this chicken running around. He was the manager of the Club. They were having a costume dance that night. And, of course, that chicken did what chickens tend to do when they get excited. And it was a mess. [1]

Peter Haas, Sr. ('45) remembered these antics too. He and George Wilson would *"steal chickens and let them loose during fancy dances at the Mountain Lakes Club. You should have heard the noise. Don't know if the chickens were louder or the women."*[1]

Skip Watts moves on to the church bell story…

We were just one of the many generations that got to it. A year or two after [the chicken episode] we decided to steal the bell from the Community Church. So, we climbed up in the bell tower, unloosened it, lowered it down with a rope and when it set on the floor the bell was so flat that we couldn't get our fingers underneath it and we couldn't rock it. So, we had to leave the bell in the bell tower-down at the floor of the bell tower. And we got caught. Harry Dennis was police chief at the time. We were out walking home figuring-very proud of ourselves that we'd done this. He came up behind us with his car, tooted his horn and just said one thing, "Get in." So, we did get in and he took us down to the jail, which at that time was down off Romaine Road. And we spent the night in jail. He called my parents and my father said, "Lock the door. Let him stay there overnight." Then Harry got nervous and went out to Paul's Diner and bought us hamburgers. [1]

Some were perpetrators while others staunchly defended their territories. Tom Stewart ('72) recalls

Protecting our house on Mischief Night with garden hoses and eggs and watching mobs of 7th graders, 8th graders, etc.… walk by and not consider messing with our house. As a kid in junior-high at the time and being the oldest in the family I felt a sense of pride and accomplishment that no one messed with our house.[3]

Sister Amy Stewart-Wilmarth ('74) chimes in:

It was so much fun to collect the acorns in paper bags and then hide behind our stone wall waiting for the high school kids to come by. We had a system—the family next door had hoses and would signal when kids came down the street from that end, and then we would signal if they came up the hill. Gus Reynolds ('75) lived across the street and had eggs. So, when the signal was sounded, we all hid ready with our weapons of water, acorns and eggs and if any high school kids came on to any of our properties, we would bombard them with water, acorns and eggs! I only remember it happening once and that high school kid chased Gus after being hit with an egg! But Gus outran him I believe. Our parents were fine with us doing this so long as we stayed on our property and because we were protecting our houses![3]

The Stewart battle station at 92 Laurel Hill Road.

Whether you were participants—"mischievers"—or protectors of your castle, there was always a tale to tell at school the next day. Once the tales were told, it was on to sharing last minute Halloween costume ideas and strategies to cover the entire town in hopes of two pillowcases full of candy!

Halloween

Halloween traditions started at an early age. The first memory for most was the Halloween parade at school. Dressed in our favorite costume or

Pumpkin Harvest, Jane & Jim Barnes, 105 Kenilworth Road.

character, we paraded around the Lake Drive school yard while others enjoyed the long-standing tradition of marching around the football field by Wildwood School. Another decades-long tradition was going to the school to bob for apples. Frank Wiswall (b. 1919) remembers Halloween from his youth. *"They used to open up the gym in the public school and they had big basins down there with apples. You could bob for apples. And costumes...you'd make your own costume."*[1]

Bobbing for apples at the school lasted through the 1960s, ending either at the behest of a germaphobe or just falling out of fashion. In our day, Halloween meant home-made treats, especially the popcorn balls from North Crane Road and performing some sort of trick or entertainment to get a treat.

Halloween involves strategy and stamina if you want to traverse the entire town. First, avoid roads with long stretches without any houses. Second, use pillowcases which are more durable than paper grocery bags, especially on those rainy Halloween nights. Third, if friends have to be in early, save your own neighborhood for last. It's safe enough to navigate alone. Other rules include: a) don't buy a costume (like your parents are actually going to do that!), make your own; and b) if you're a teenager, wear a costume and don't be a jerk—you'll still get candy. Taking younger brothers and sisters out trick-or-treating will earn you extra points too!

Thanksgiving

Thanksgiving was a quieter holiday shared with family. There were two exceptions to that—the *"Thanksgiving breakfast at the Community Church put on by Beulah Littell"* (James Barnes, '51) and in later years, the Mountain Lakes vs Morris Catholic game played Thanksgiving morning. (It is football, after all!).

10:00 am: Dress up and go to MLHS vs. Morris Catholic football game

1:00 pm: Head to Grandma and Grandpa's house for Thanksgiving meal. Creamed pearl onions made once a year for Grandpa, cornbread sage dressing, Aunt Jane making the gravy, and Grandma forgetting the rolls and burning them. Lounging around with bellies full while watching the only TV in the basement den. When the sun set it was time for turkey sandwiches on white toast with a thick schmear of Miracle Whip!

Fall's Kaleidoscope

Growing Up Laker in the fall evokes many memories—school, football, holidays—all of which take place against a gorgeous backdrop of colors. Our senses are assaulted with the sights of incredible jewel-toned leaves, the sounds of rustling leaves and crunching acorns, and the sight of smoke billowing up from fires in an ancient dance. We walk around the lakes, traverse the town from Tower Hill to the Village, and stroll from Del's Village in Boonton to Paul's Diner on Route 46 along the Boulevard. Trails through the woods fill with the fragrance of fall—earthy and damp—especially after the rain. We see leaves of apple red, lemon yellow, orange, nutmeg, and cinnamon. The colors are especially magnificent when reflected off the smooth-as-glass waters of our many lakes. Daytime colors are beautiful; nighttime skies are simply stunning. The skies of fall have an intensity and clarity like no other season. What is more perfect than lying in the front yard, looking up at the harvest moon or a canvas of stars? We are transported even if just for a moment to a place of unbounded peace and possibilities. We barely have our Thanksgiving meal digested when a fierce Nor'easter jolts us out of our reverie and announces, "Winter is here!"

My Favorite Fall Memories

(What's in your fall kaleidoscope of Growing Up Laker?)

Winter
Chapter Two

The frenzied days of December mark the start of winter in Mountain Lakes. We pore over the Sears, JC Penney, and Montgomery Ward catalogs making our Christmas wish lists. We include the page numbers to make sure Santa gets it right. Parents and older kids scramble to

complete holiday tasks. Christmas music programs mark the official start of the school break. We gather with friends to carol around town. Weekends fill up quickly—parents are off to their adult parties and scramble to find babysitters for us. We teens are babysitting or working the adult parties, serving hors d'oeuvres and drinks to our parents' guests. Finally, we journey into New York City to see the store window Christmas scenes, the Christmas tree lighting, and skating at Rockefeller Center. If we're lucky, we might see the Rockettes at Radio City Music Hall!

At school, we prepare for the annual Christmas chorus and band concert, complete with beautiful solos. A group is scouring the town for pine boughs to decorate the stage. The band has wrapped up its Christmas tree fundraiser. Some organization is selling Christmas wreaths. The lighting of the town Christmas tree takes center stage. Dads dress up as Santa and visit nearby friends and extended families. Churches host their annual Christmas Bazaars with homemade pies and other delights.

Christmas vacation arrives! We race to buy family gifts at Del's Village, in Denville, or hitch a ride to Rockaway Mall. Some of the favorites include Whitman's Sampler box of chocolates for 25 cents and a new tube of lipstick for Mom. And when money is tight, we put our purchases on the drug store charge account. We save up for a nice lunch then dress up and ride the bus to Morristown. We shop at Epstein's and find last minute gifts at Woolworths. We might even suffer a trip with mom to Short Hills Mall. We go with parents or walk all the way to Grace Lord Park in Boonton to see Santa. When we get older, we still get a thrill when Santa drives by on the firetruck. We tag along with little brothers and sisters to visit him at the firehouse.

The closer we get to Christmas, the quieter the nights, the clearer the skies, the brighter the stars. We walk along the streets with friends, often in complete silence and take in the holiday lights. Then someone breaks the silence and suggests caroling. Off we go house to house singing Christmas carols and hoping someone remembers the words to Good King Wenceslas. Yes, the spirit of Christmas descends upon us.

Winter

Something magical happens. When Christmas Eve arrives, churches open their doors even wider, the handbells chime, candle lights burn bright, and voices sing out in joyous harmony. The singing of O Holy Night brings a tear to our eye. Afterwards, we try to walk all the way home with our candle still aglow. We gather with family and friends this night, often ending up at Midnight Mass at Saint Catherine's Church. The mass is in Latin and acolytes and grownups alike try to stay awake.

On Christmas morning, we gather at the top of the stairs to await the go-ahead to discover the gifts that Santa has left. But first…Dad blinds us with the movie camera lights to capture the moment. Or, we pose on the stairway for an annual family Christmas photo and are blinded by the still camera light bulb. Either way, stunned by the brightness, we stagger down the steps and into the living room to see the Christmas glory.

Once the Christmas break ends, it's back to school. The only community activity that breaks up the winter chill is basketball. Sports fans move indoors from the fields to the gym basketball court. The wooden bleachers pull out from the walls and the refreshment stand lines the entryway. We shake off the cold, shed our winter garb, climb the bleachers, and root our team on. The gym reverberates with the pounding of feet on the bleachers, synchronized clapping led by cheerleaders, the squeal of players' sneakers on the highly polished floors, and the jolt of the scoreboard buzzer. The players sit on the far side of the gym, focused on their coach and the game. The fast action on the court contrasts with the seemingly slow pace of football.

Our basketball teams fared well over the decades; however, the 1960s and 1970s were the golden age of Laker basketball for my generation. Under the leadership of George Wilson, Laker teams won all sorts of championships. The most notable seasons boasted Group I titles in 1962 (with an undefeated season of 25-0) and 1969. The Lakers went on to claim the first Morris County Tournament basketball title in 1970, and in 1971 the team captured the North 2 Group II title. *"Known for teams that played with unbridled passion and disciplined precision, Coach Wilson helped establish an athletic tradition at Mountain Lakes High School the likes of which the small Morris County town had never seen"* (George Wilson Obituary 2017). Although basketball took center court as a community spectator sport, let's not forget our school swimming and diving teams.

Now you'd think after spending an entire summer swimming and diving in competitions a few times a week, Laker kids would have had their fill. Nope. With the start of the school year, they moved their activities indoors. Early on practicing for meets was no simple logistical feat. With no indoor pool of our own until the Lakeland Hills YMCA was built in 1974, the team travelled to distant facilities to practice and compete. Other challenges were arising as well, like how to accommodate girls on the team.

The high school swim and dive program was the first to welcome girls to a high school team. My mother likes to tell the story of girls taking the swim program by storm in the early 1970s. My sister Kathy Barnes and her classmates Kim Brown, Amy Hogeboom, and Wendy Navin—all from the class of 1977—were summer swim team powerhouses. When they joined a few other girls on the boys' high school swim team, they made even more waves. Travelling to meets, the girls changed clothes in restrooms since there were no locker room accommodations for them. Entering the pool area, they were met with snickers and side comments from boys on the other teams. That quickly ended once the gals left them sputtering in their wake. The swimming and diving teams carried over their summer success to conquer a new set of adversaries. Once again, whether it's swimming or basketball, we leave it to the team members, statisticians, sports historians, and other devoted fans to fill you in on facts and specific events.

Outdoor Adventures

Beyond the gymnasium walls, winter signals time for good old-fashioned fun! It's a time to try on last year's skates and skis, hope for new ones for Christmas, and pray for lots of snow days. It's a time of sledding down the hills and hoping you don't cross the Boulevard or other

Winter

intersections where cars dare to drive. It's hoping the ice is safe so you don't sink as you fly off the back yard and crash onto the lake. It's walking home from school across the lakes free from the booming sound of ice cracking. In essence, there were really only three things you had to master *Growing Up Laker* in winter: 1) skating, 2) sledding down steep hills, and 3) navigating the slippery byways while WALKING everywhere. (Yes, we're still walking. Not even the icy winter winds could sway our parents to drive us anywhere!)

Skating across the decades on Mountain Lake, Shadown Lake, and the Cove.

Skating

Each winter as the lakes begin to freeze, families break out the skates. Old ones are polished and passed down to the next kid in line or we head to church bazaars in hopes of finding a good used pair. New ones for the oldest kid, the only kid, or for whom none of last year's skates fit. There are figure skates, hockey skates, and double-bladed skates for the toddlers.

Every Laker toddler experiences the winter rite of passage. When the flag goes up announcing the ice is safe, parents carry kitchen chair in one arm and toddler in the other to the lake and strap double-bladed skates to the designated toddler's boots. Sandwiched between parents or older siblings, the toddler begins his/her first foray into the world of Laker skating. In an hour or so, the toddler might graduate from loving hands to solo push of the kitchen chair to master the art of skating on his/her own.

I recall being only four years old and proud to be skating on single blades. It was a big deal when I skated the whole length of the Cove and Mountain Lake. It seemed half the town was out on the lake on a winter day. Where else would the town put up the red ball on the flagpole and have a special hotline to say if the lakes were safe to skate on? (Anon)[3]

The official opening of skating season was marked by the hoisting of "the flag." We'd ask our parents' permission to go skating and their reply was, "Is the flag up?" It was a practice brought about by tragedy in early times. One of the earliest residents, Ralph Wells (b. 1916) fills us in on how the tradition of testing the ice came about:

Two fellows, McEwan, who lived down on Pollard Road, and Streeter who lived on Morris right near Midvale…took bicycles and went out on the lake and went through the ice and drowned. And that was the start of putting a flag up on the lake, a white flag with a red ball in the center. Harry Dennis [the police chief] used to test that lake, and make sure it was safe for skating.[1]

David Higgins (b. 1922) adds "*At the old firehouse at the corner of Boulevard and Briarcliff Road they used to raise a flag with a white background and a red ball on it when the ice was safe. They stopped in World War II because it looked like the Japanese flag. They did the same thing at the Mountain Lakes Club.*"[1]

Bonfires, hot chocolate, music, and games were common sights and sounds on the lakes in winter. In the early days, there was curling, sailing with ice boats, and hockey. When curling went out of style, hockey took over. Ice boats disappeared and were replaced by kids with sheets or towels stretch taut to catch the wind. Bonnie Bedford Parks ('74) reminisces:

> *I took full advantage of the secluded cove on Mountain Lake right out our back door. With favorable ice conditions and a brisk wind, two girls hanging on opposite ends of a beach towel could blow down the length of the lake on figure skates, past Island Beach, all the way to the Mountain Lakes Club in less than 15 minutes.*[3]

When the ice was extremely strong, small trucks and plows would clear the snow. "*There were lights on an empty lot on Wildwood Lake controlled from the old firehouse and the music was piped from there. We had outdoor fires — that was part of my job to keep the fire burning*" (David Higgins).[1] And in the 50s, "*people would light fires and invite us to have hot chocolate. We would make enormous whips that would send people flying for a long way*" (Alice Parman, '60).[1] Throughout the decades, crack the whip endured, sending the weaker skaters flying off the tail end and getting battered and bruised along the way.

Those who lived on the lakes were fortunate. Steve McCurdy ('72) remembers winter on Mountain Lake:

> *When the lake would freeze, especially on very cold nights, you could hear the ice boom all night long and once in a while you could see ice cracks form the length of the lake when you were standing on the ice! That was very cool. One of our neighbors would often take his snowplow tractor out on the lake to clear skating paths of snow, make hockey rinks and skating areas around the lake. There was always a hockey rink in front of Jay Elder's house and for several years I 'played hockey' in sneakers until I finally learned to skate on skates!*[3]

Tom Stewart ('72) reminisces about ice hockey adventures on Wildwood Lake.

> *In the winter we would play ice hockey on Wildwood Lake. When the white flag with the large red dot was up and flying over the Boro Hall, at the time at the intersection of the Boulevard and Briarcliff, we would go out with 2x4s and snow shovels to build our rink! We usually ended up near the dike across the street from Wildwood Elementary. It was more open, no trees on the shoreline, and the wind usually did a good job clearing off any new fallen snow. The trick was not to lift the puck, otherwise it would clear the 2x4s and sail across the lake!*

And on the Cove, Beth Tunnell Howard ('83) recalls how some things just never change…except perhaps for team composition.

> *In classic ML style, there were impromptu, pick-up hockey games most days and anyone could jump in: girls and boys spanning a vast array of ages. Because we lived right there, inevitably I'd have a large pack of kids follow me into the house for hot chocolate and snacks. Mom never complained. We'd leave a dozen pair of skates with melting ice on her hardwood floors in the entrance hall and make a huge mess in the kitchen.[3]*

Nothing said Laker winter like the smell of wool mittens, hats and scarves thawing out—then drying out—on the hot radiators. And nothing rivals the race up the stairs on hands and knees with skates still on to get to the bathroom on time. Oh, those were the times we wished our Hapgood homes came with first floor bathrooms!

While many had the speed, power, and grace to master all things skating, the rest of us were content to make it from point A to point B without falling. I couldn't skate like my other friends—I could go forward and backward, but nothing else. I used to cross the street at night and skate under the stars. I would pretend I was Peggy Fleming even though jumping or twirling were outside my skill set. Afterward, I'd lie down on the ice, look up at the stars, and disappear into the mystery of the universe.

The frozen lakes offered another important advantage to Laker kids—short cuts to our destination. For 60 years—from Myrtle Hillman

Kingsley to Beth Tunnell Howard traversing the frozen lakes was standard practice. Myrtle Hillman Kingsley tells it like this:

My brother and I would skate from our end of the lake to school [Mountain Lake, near Crane Road, to Lake Drive School]. You know, in the olden days you didn't have shoe skates, you had good, sturdy Buster Brown oxfords, and you just put the skates on and skated to school. And you put them in your locker and that was fine.[1]

For Beth, "I had a short cut riding my bike or walking to school—it was such fun to simply ride across the lake and bypass the circuitous street route!"[3]

Entrance to the Sled Run from Overlook Road.

Sledding

Coasting, sleigh riding, or sledding—barreling down insanely steep hills at break-neck speed—was the order of the day when Laker kids weren't skating. We flew down roads, hills in the woods, and back yards over stone walls. Then we climbed the hills and did it again. The most popular routes include North Briarcliff and North Glen Road

with all its connecting roads, Pollard Road, and the Hillcrest to Midvale circuit. Neighborhood kids used the trail between Overlook Road and Tower Hill which was turned it into an official sled run in the 1960s. Of course, nothing said easy sledding like down your own back yard through the neighbors' yards until some natural barrier stopped your ride. Finally, when parents felt adventurous or benevolent, they took us to enjoy the hills behind St. Clare's Hospital.

Our early residents remember coasting on Pollard Road and with friends down Addington (North Glen) Road starting at the water tower. Some Laker kids made their stops in friends' driveways while others kept on going; speeding down North Glen, across the Boulevard to points beyond. Jack Lee (b. ca 1910) used to sled *"down Hillcrest to Midvale and Midvale all the way to Intervale Road. And then* [on] *Pollard we used to go down Pollard Road most of the way to well beyond Rockaway Terrace."* Over on North Glen, he would *"start at Crestview Road…go down Mt. Addington…right on across the Boulevard and almost to Melrose."*[1]

Coasting, sleigh riding, and sledding wasn't just for kids, though. In early days, adults would pile into large sleighs that held eight to ten people. With steering rudder in hand, the adults would race down the hills too. Thirty years later, folks were still flying down those roads. Alice Parman ('60) remembers *"sleigh riding, mostly on Glen Road, which would be officially closed to traffic so everyone could go sleigh riding (that's what we called it, not sledding)."*[1]

While some of the hillside roads closed for sledding, the Boulevard was not. So, you'd better have a plan to stave off disaster in the event your sled gained enough momentum to cross the Boulevard. David Higgins remembers the town putting gravel and cinders on the road to stop the sleds and prevent them from going onto the Boulevard. Another more common tactic for surviving a perilous ride was to station someone down at the Boulevard. *"They stopped cars* [and] *warned the kids so they could ditch the sleds instead of going across the road."*[1] There were giant snow angels watching over Laker kids in winter. Thank goodness for bulky winter clothing that prevented broken bones and bruised bodies as we bailed out at the bottom of the hills.

Skiing

Skiing was another Laker winter staple. Kids often began their ski careers in back yards or down the same streets as the sledders. Families paid for lessons at Craigmeur; their children gently tumbling down the hills as they mastered the snowplow, then scrambling back up with rope tows and T-bars. Once graduated, many moved on to the slopes of Great Gorge and out-of-town venues in New Hampshire and Vermont. The high school ski club and ski team spent their time at Great Gorge as well. Great Gorge opened in 1965, and with the addition of the Playboy Club in 1972, it was the hottest thing going for Laker kids. It seemed an odd place for a high school ski club, but it was the '70s after all. It's difficult for outsiders to imagine a mid-winter break from school, but we had one and it seemed designed specifically for the skiing families in town.

Winter wasn't just about skating, sledding, and skiing. We built snowmen and snow horses, erected snow forts complete with tunnels, and had snowball fights. We stashed snowballs in the freezer to have on hand for epic neighborhood battles. It was a time of gathering around the radio to listen to school closures and waiting for them to call out *"all Mountain Lakes public schools…it was always one of the last schools"* (Peg Bonyata, '74).[3]

Faith Witham Robertson recalls the blizzard of '47.

It was the day after Christmas. It was 26 inches of snow. And a week later we had an ice storm on top of it. I was scheduled for surgery and was able to get to the hospital, so I was out of the house when the ice storm came. I got home a couple days after. But that was a monstrous storm. The ice was so thick it was bending the branches down.[1]

We had our share of snowstorms, but it seemed ice storms were more common, felling mighty oak trees and creating bowered pathways along the Boulevard sidewalk between Overlook and Laurel Hill Roads. Residents who lived around the lakes and along streets where birch trees were abundant experienced the same sights.

Robert E. Lee Barnes House, 126 Pollard Road.

Winter was also a curious time in our big Hapgood homes, especially for those of us who slept on the third floor. Remember the clanking and whistling of the radiators as they strained to push heat and steam up to our room? We slept under layers of blankets, invited siblings and dogs to join us to stay warm, and scraped the frost off the inside of the windows on frigid morns. We battled with brothers and sisters over who got to put their clothes on the radiators overnight. Despite all those chilly days and nights, winter in Mountain Lakes was a marvelous time for kids *Growing Up Laker*. Eventually we'd put away our skates and sleds and wait for the first signs of spring.

92 Laurel Hill Road.

Winter's Kaleidoscope

Our winter memories return us to days of frozen fingers and toes, the joy and burden of lugging sleds up steep hills for 15 minutes only to soar down them in less than three. We bundle up little brothers and sisters, head out to the lakes, then discover they need to use the bathroom. We inhale the fragrance of wet woolen clothes on the radiators, our indoor and outdoor fires, fresh cut boughs to decorate our homes, and homemade cookies of the season. Excepting Christmas lights, we are surrounded by shades of black and white. Occasionally we are blessed with a crisp and clear day, blinded by blue skies and silvery mirror-like lawns. Squeals and peals of laughter echo throughout the town as we race down snowy hills on our sleds. Occasionally the boom of expanding ice rattles our nerves. We embrace the spirit of winter fun, share good times around the fireplace with family and friends. We give thanks for a great start to the new year and await spring's arrival!

My Favorite Winter Memories
(What's in your winter kaleidoscope of Growing Up Laker?)

Spring
Chapter Three

Spring assaults our senses with rebirth! It washes away the drab black, white, grays, and browns and releases dabs of early color. New green leaves begin to pop from the bare branches. Early bloomers like hyacinths and crocuses spring up to say hello. The sky is bluer, the grass is greener. Even the air smells different. No longer frozen—as if smells can freeze—the woods smell new and welcoming. The lakes beckon us to their thawed shores, lure us in with whispered breezes. We open windows to let in spring air and chase away winter congestion. We dig into the earth to begin planting flowers and vegetables. The soil is cold, yet ready to receive new seeds and bulbs. The robins have returned and fill the air with their song. If we are lucky, we spy baby rabbits and deer in the woods.

Spring in Mountain Lakes—a curious collection of starts and finishes. Basketball is over and so is cheerleading. Spring training for baseball, track, and other sports is starting up. Late season snowstorms catch us off guard. Families are getting ready for the second school break of the year. Skiing in February, sunning in the islands in April. For those of us not so fortunate, hanging out around at home with friends and family.

Tell-tale signs that spring is near include puddles and slush on the frozen lakes. We leap over the brittle ice along the water's edge in hopes of finding solid surfaces. More often though, we end up with cold wet feet and abandon our cherished frozen lake short-cuts until next winter. Our other shortcuts aren't much better in the spring thaw. We take the long way home to avoid the muddy shortcuts across lawns, fields, and through the woods. To a Laker kid, it takes forever for the winter snows to evaporate and spring carpets to emerge. When impatience wins out, we pay for it with muddy shoes, wet socks, and mother's disapproval ("Take those shoes off before coming in the house!"). We still bundle up on chilly mornings, then find ourselves burdened by the weight of winter coats under the afternoon sun. We forget our winter wear at school or the playground; Mom sends us back to retrieve them ("We paid good money for those."). Against this backdrop of emerging spring are four main highlights of Growing Up Laker: GAA, Trout Derby, Memorial Day, and Graduation.

It's March... Do You Feel It? G... A... A!

Pick your captains. Pick the show. Pick your team. Tryout for tumbling, marching, tap, Danish, modern. Cover classroom windows during practice. Build the routines. Sew your costumes. Write team songs. Paint sets in cold garages. Stay up all night. Hang banners off second story balconies. Paint the rock. Eat at team spaghetti dinners. Eat at team breakfasts. Eat too many Dunkin' Donuts. Wake up the town with Friday morning motorcades. Keep them up with all night

Spring

parties! Two and a half months of commotion building to a frenzy by mid-May. Even teachers are distracted by then.

GAA—More Than Just a Show

The Girls' Athletic Association (GAA) has a wonderful history. The following excerpts were gleaned from Mountain Lakes High School Yearbooks. GAA makes its debut in the 1939 MLHS Yearbook:

This year, after much heated discussion, the Boys' and Girls' Athletic Associations merged into The Mountain Lakes High School Athletic Association. This new arrangement has worked out very well, with the girls taking care of the cheer leading and the candy concession at all of the home games. (34)

Apparently, cheering and sitting in the concession stand wasn't enough to satisfy the girls' desire for athletic pursuits. By 1948, the GAA was back, reconceived by Miss Dorothy Hicinbothem.

Through the G.A.A., it has been possible for the girls to participate in inter-scholastic competition. For the second year, the class of '48 held the hockey championship for intramural competition. Girls' basketball proved to be quite successful this season…the Seniors won the majority of the basketball games. Several new activities such as horseback riding, tumbling, archery, and modern dance were introduced. (60)

The purpose of the GAA was *"to promote participation in girls' athletics in a sportsman-like manner, to foster a feeling of class spirit in intra-mural programs, and to uphold a high standard of school spirit in inter-scholastic competition."* (1949 MLHS Yearbook). This intramural program consisted of Orange and Blue teams competing against each other in various sports. The spring GAA Sports Night highlighted the activities the girls participated in throughout the schoolyear.

The GAA continued to grow in its ability to provide opportunities to girls in intramural sports and proving itself to be resilient and flexible in many ways. In 1955, *"when the hockey season was unexpectedly shortened by the polio quarantine, the girls turned their effort to basketball, softball, and to their annual Sports Night... G.A.A. is an important activity to the girls of Mountain Lakes High School"* (1955 MLHS Yearbook).

Sports Night continued to grow as the main attraction of the GAA. It's success and popularity grew such that by 1960, the Orange and Blue Show was held on two consecutive nights. However, by the 1990s, girls' sports had expanded in variety and grown in membership. The GAA Show had outlived its purpose and came to the end of an era. The 1997 Yearbook gave tribute to the GAA:

The End of an Era G. A. A. 1948-1996...G.A.A. has been a vital part of Mountain Lakes High School since its introduction in 1948. The annual March show has become for some, a highlight of the school year, for others, a dreaded and unnecessary bother. In past years, rumors have circulated about the possibility to end the MLHS tradition, but it was only this year that the possibility seems to have become a reality. Due to a general lack of enthusiasm, there was no show presented this year. Some felt that this decision was a tragedy, others welcomed it without hesitation. (122)

The GAA show, as it was called in the late 1960s until its retirement in 1997, was the hallmark of sisterhood, leadership and teamwork. It was a family affair, the captainship often passing from one sister to another. Rivals for three months out of the year, friends for a lifetime. The GAA fever lasted until Mother's Day weekend (in our day, anyway). And sandwiched in middle of this GAA frenzy came another Laker tradition...

Trout Derby

It's mid-April and we all know what that means...TROUT DERBY! Each year since 1963, the Trout Derby has been bringing families and friends together for a few short hours and making memories that last a lifetime. Whether you cared about fishing or not, Trout Derby was the place to be on that Saturday in April. So many ways to win a prize: catch the Golden Trout, the first trout, the largest trout, a tagged trout. Then of course you had to clean and eat them. Freezers filled up and it

Memories of Trout Derby at the Propagation Pond (Cove) and Birchwood Lake.

seemed every meal for a while consisted of trout…baked trout, grilled trout, trout over an open campfire.

During the first few years, the Trout Derby was held at the pond on the Boulevard between Overlook Road and North Crane Road. Named the Cove on local maps, we called it Propagation Pond. The Trout Derby became such a success that by 1969, it was moved to Birchwood Lake to provide more shoreline for the burgeoning crowds.

Although the Trout Derby lasted a few short hours on a cool Saturday morning, the preparations and anticipation of the day were much longer. Talk at the dinner table and on the schoolyards took on a life of its own—the bets, the goals, the bait, the best spots. Digging out the fishing gear and practicing casting in the yard had a sense of urgency. While families and kids plotted their strategies, the Trout Derby organizers were hard at work too. Publicizing the event and buying the trout and prizes was easy. Stocking the lake required a bit more effort. The truck from the hatchery rolled up to the water's edge. Volunteers carefully scooped the trout out of large barrels and released them into the lake. In the early hours around dawn on the day of the event, those same organizers readied the registration desk and snack shack for the onslaught of excited and hungry anglers.

Veteran anglers dress the part: fishing hat, lots of layers for the cold and rain—jacket, windbreaker, sweatshirt with hood and pockets, boots, warm socks. On the occasional warm April morning they survive with jeans and a t-shirt! They carry rods and reels, tackle boxes and creels ready to use whatever it takes to land the big one.

Ambitious and adventurous anglers camp out the night before to mark their favorite spot. They stay up all night long swapping stories, tending to the campfire and making sure their line is in the water at the earliest possible second. They brave the cold, the rain, and one year snow to get a coveted fishing spot. Chris McGovern muses *"How a bunch of 12-year-olds never burned those woods down is still mystifying."*[4] Others show up hours early to stake their claim along the shores. Some believe the right-hand side of the lake holds the most promise (close to camping areas anyway), but others swear by the left-side banks beyond the beach.

The debate over the perfect bait is a popular topic. Do we use lures, white bread rolled up in balls, those slimy orange eggs in the narrow glass jars, beef liver, or nightcrawlers and their inferior cousins—the common worm—dug up in the middle of the night, or a commercial lure? Anglers had their bait of choice and the trout seemed to have their favorites that varied from year to year too.

When it is all said and done, kids line up to claim their prizes—prizes for the first fish, largest fish, tagged fish and the coveted Golden Trout. What do we win? Fishing poles, creels, tackle boxes, gift certificates, and fish encyclopedias, all presented by derby officials accompanied by a photo op and handshake with the Mayor. Bonnie Bedford Park recalls: *"I won a rod and a creel. Caught five fish in 27 minutes. My dad Buz knew where the best hole was."*[4] The local paper is there every year to capture the joy of kids, friends, and family participating in this

Spring

Mountain Lakes Rod & Gun Club

BOX 71 • MOUNTAIN LAKES, NEW JERSEY

February 22, 1964

BONNIE BEDFORD -- 1963
MOUNTAIN LAKES NEWS

Dear Mountain Laker:

The first Mountain Lakes Trout Derby for juniors was held at Cove Lake on April 6, 1963. 230 boys and girls participated. You helped buy the trout.

The juniors want a derby in 1964. Will you again help buy the trout? A dollar (or more) in the enclosed envelope is the kind of help needed.

If senior response to this plea is sufficient the derby will be held at Cove Lake on Saturday, April 11. Trout stocked would be worm loving "Brookies" and at least 80% will be caught that day.

The fishing season could again get off to a rousing start for we estimate 260 girls and boys would take part in a trout derby this year.

Won't you too please participate TODAY?

Cordially,

1964 TROUT DERBY COMMITTEE

VES HOFFMAN • BOB LEBO • JOHN HESS • GEORGE LILIEHOLM • BRUCE AINSWORTH • JOHN MASSON • JOHN WALDRON
BOB NORTON • HERB BARNES • GLEN SCUTT • ED PEABODY

Laker tradition. My youngest sister Jennifer had her photo in one of the local newspapers when she was about three years old. She's holding her trout and has a black eye! Three years later in 1973, she is back again in the *Times-Bulletin* with her string of fish and another proud and happy angler—Bruce Merritt—who caught the Golden Trout!

Before we know it, the Trout Derby is over, but the quest for prized trout continues throughout the season. The excitement returns when we catch the coveted Golden Trout and the larger ones that eluded us during the derby. Brothers shake their heads when younger sisters best them!

Naturally with every fishing event comes a fish story. Rusty Helff shared his story: The Legend of the Golded Trout.

One year about three months after the Derby, my sister asked to borrow one of my poles to go fishing. She was going to dig up worms for bait. I reminded her I had used every bait known to a trout and there was no way a simple worm would catch a trout out of that lake, but off she went. When I got home that evening, she told me she had caught one. To my surprise, inside [the basket] was THE MOTHER OF ALL TROUTS—at least 24 inches with a tag in its mouth. That is when I realized [the legend] was ALL real. The monster trout was not just a fisherman's tale. (Facebook Post, 2018)

We'll pause now so you can share your favorite Trout Derby fish tale.

The Trout Derby was and is the embodiment of community spirit, family tradition, and friendly competition. Lakers share bait, untangle each other's lines, and for a few short hours get lost in the experience of just being. Fishing has much to teach kids about time...and patience...and payoff. Our time spent as kids fishing either once a year or every day of the year teaches us valuable lessons. We learn sportsmanship, a philosophy of living, and a sincere respect and appreciation for the natural resources that surround us.

Sometime between Trout Derby and GAA it was time for the annual changing of the windows. You remember—take down the storm windows and put up the screens. We were lucky. Our windows were numbered and so were the screens and storm windows. After a thorough washing, it was a matter of matching them to the correct window and hoisting them up to my father to install. Thirty windows that I can count. Of course, there were more before the front porch was screened in and later converted to a TV room.

Spring

Memorial Day

The Memorial Day Parade and ceremony at Memorial Park wrap up spring and usher in hopes of a great summer. The parade starts on Briarcliff Road, traverses along the Boulevard and turns down Lake Drive Road to Memorial Park. All the scout troops in town march in the parade along with the high school band. Other organizations join in. Kids decorate their bicycles and ride along. Parade participants form up in the grassy area along the Canal and important grownups give speeches. I don't recall the speeches, but I do recall the solemnity with which the ceremony took place. It was one of the few non-athletic events that brought the town together.

Long-time resident Tim Delchamps gave the Memorial Day speech in 1994. Here are a few excerpts courtesy of his sons Steven and David Delchamps.

Fifty years ago, next Monday, American, British, and Canadian airborne assaults behind enemy lines began the Battle of Normandy. It was approximately 1:30 AM on the sixth of June. Five hours later Allied ground troops stormed ashore on five separate fronts along a 60-mile stretch of Normandy coastline. By the end of the day, the five beachheads had been secured by 156,000 Allied fighting men and six days later all five fronts were linked. By July 19th, with the seizing of the St. Lo by the U.S. First Army, and Caen by the British Second Army, the first phase of the Normandy Campaign was over.

Mr. Delchamps continued his speech:

Each year we come together in this lovely setting with a common purpose bring with us our individual collection of thoughts and memories of people and times past; especially thoughts and memories of those we knew all too briefly. It is in their names that we come to renew and re-dedicate our hopes for future generations. On each occasion, standing where you stand now, I've wondered how my own thoughts and feelings compare with those of others. Since such reflections are the personal and private possession of each of us, this curiosity must remain largely unsatisfied. Nevertheless, it is both my privilege and my pleasure to turn the problem around today and to share my thoughts and feelings with you.

Mr. Delchamps went on to share the stories of many veterans including the ones whose names are on the bronze plaque in the park. He concluded his remarks with a tribute to those who never returned. Every Memorial Day a new speaker shares his or her tributes to those who gave the ultimate sacrifice. The only thing that changes over the years is the addition of more names to the list.

Spring

WWI and WWII Memorial Stones at the Memorial Park.

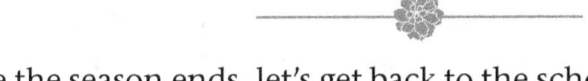

Before the season ends, let's get back to the school yard. We spent time in the fall and winter talking about football and basketball, but we'd be remiss if we didn't pay homage to other sports such as cross country, baseball, and track. Granted, we're not sports historians and scouring the high school yearbooks gave few details about these spring sports as publishing timelines seemed to get in the way. If I recall correctly, these sports took place right after school, so the scheduling didn't lend itself to a large fan base like football and basketball. Nonetheless, they were still instrumental in molding teenagers into responsible young adults. From the first days of the Mountain Lakes High School, boys' sports programs grew and excelled.

Baseball first showed up on the scene in 1938. The Briarcliff High School was brand new, so games were played on Neafie's Field (more on that place later). Albeit there is little information available in the

yearbooks, we do see great success in the 1950s. George Wilson's return to Mountain Lakes in 1960 ensured the legacy of great baseball continued throughout his coaching career resulting in a variety of championship seasons along the way. Mountain Lakes High School baseball produced a couple notable players. After college *"George Wilson was drafted by the Milwaukee Braves organization and ultimately reached the highest levels of their Minor League system as a right-handed pitcher"* (George Wilson Obituary, 2017). Another notable was lefthand pitcher Dave Bishop ('69) who was drafted by the California Angels in the 1969 MLB June Amateur Draft, the Philadelphia Phillies in the 1971 MLB January Draft-Secondary Phase, and the New York Yankees in the 1st round (17th) of the 1971 MLB June Draft-Secondary Phase (baseball-reference.com).

Cross Country makes its debut in Mountain Lakes High School in 1945 completing its first season with an undefeated dual meet record. The harriers go on to have many more championship seasons over the next 40 years. One of the most poignant characterizations of cross country shows up in the 1969 MLHS Yearbook:

> *When a boy goes out for cross-country, he does not expect large crowds, marching bands or instant fame. What he anticipates is a season of endless toil, sweat, and sacrifice. But it is the type of sport that provides rewards in the way of self-satisfaction, in knowing that you have done your best. Any runner always says that his greatest competitor is himself. Rain, sleet or cold do not deter the disciplined efforts of a runner to improve his time. No, cross-country is not glamorous to the spectator, but to the athlete the rewards of self-improvement are more important.* (65)

Finally, spring of 1940 brought an invitation for boys to join the high school's newly formed track team. The 1940 MLHS Yearbook notes:

> *With only two or three members of the track squad who have had any previous running experience, it is impossible to predict or to be too hopeful with respect to the probable success of the team's first*

Spring

season of competition. However, unlike baseball, track stars can be developed in a single season and we are hoping for the best. (39)

It turns out "the best" is what they got over the next few years. The cindermen of the 1940s are engaged throughout the year, not just in springtime. They improve exponentially, setting records and winning championships along the way, and all this without the convenience of a track of their own. The 1943 MLHS Yearbook highlights the accomplishments of the track team:

Many of the boys on this year's team had the advantage of training and experience of cross-country last fall and competition in the National Interscholastic meet in Madison Square Garden in Feb.... Several school records have already been broken and it looks as if more are to follow. Tom Stewart is burning up the track in the 100 and 220 yard dashes.... Skippy Watts has added 3-1/2 feet to the discus record. Although he has yet to break McEwen's record in the shot put, Red Shults is undefeated in the event. (46)

Dubbed the "trackless wonders" throughout the 1940s, the MLHS track team overcame spartan conditions to win championships, including the Penn Relays, and set the bar for track generations to come. Amy's father, Tom Stewart (mentioned in the '43 yearbook quote above) wrote in his memoirs, *"The New York Times had an article about 'the trackless wonders.' We had no track and used to practice in the streets around the high school. We beat schools such as Morristown, Dover, Roxbury and Caldwell. In my senior year, 1943, I had a county record in the 100-yard dash."*

And once again we leave it to the team members, statisticians, sports historians, and other devoted fans to fill you in on facts and specific events throughout the decades. Suffice it to say, without the likes of influential and visionary coaches such as Bill Kogen, George Wilson and Doug Wilkins, and many others who came before and after them, Mountain Lakes High School would not have achieved the athletic success and acclaim that it has.

Growing Up Laker

Tom Stewart ('43) setting track record (top). Tom's varsity letter and medals (bottom).

Graduation

On high school graduation night in mid-June, seniors file into the auditorium, girls in white gowns and boys in blue. Down the center aisle they proceed, split off at the apron of the stage—girls to the right and boys to the left—climb the stairs and file to their assigned seats. Their attention is not on the speakers but on the multitude of emotions and thoughts racing through their minds. They are excited and nervous about what lies ahead. They are thinking about how they will miss friends and familiar routines. They are thankful the days of being picked on and teased are over. Speeches conclude, diplomas are handed out, and near the end, we all stand to sing the Mountain Lakes High School Alma Mater.

The Alma Mater
Mountain Lakes High School

(Words by George H. Littell, Music by Ted Milkey)

When all Mountain Lakers gather
It is never very long
Till we praise our Alma Mater
With a song.
As we join our hearts together
Raise our voices clear and true
In allegiance to the orange
And the blue!
Sing! Sing! The Mountain Lakers' song
To thee, our loyal hearts belong
For no matter where we wander
Or wherever we may roam
We will always think of Mountain Lakes as home!
Where the echoes from the hillsides
Ring around the Wildwood Shore
Dwell a host of friends we'll cherish evermore
Though our paths may someday sever
We'll recall the happy throng
That was bound as one together in a song.
Sing! Sing! The Mountain Lakers' song
To thee, our loyal hearts belong
For no matter where we wander
Or wherever we may roam
We will always think of Mountain Lakes as home!

Kim Westfall Cayes kindly gave us permission to share excerpts from her story about her great aunt and uncle, Beulah and George Littell. George Littell is the author of the Mountain Lakes Alma Mater.

The Man Behind the Alma Mater - George Littell

Where to begin? My earliest recollection of Uncle George was in the summer of 1964 when I (age eight) my brother Randy Westfall (11), and sister Lisle Westfall Pepe (six), all dressed up as people used to do for plane trips back then, walked from the plane that had flown us from our California home, to live with our Uncle George and Aunt Beulah in Mtn. Lakes. The hot, humid air—something I'd never experienced before—hit me in the face, nearly smothering me. When we walked into the airport, we saw an elderly couple; Uncle George in a gray suit and Aunt Beulah in a blue dress and white gloves. As they drove us to their home on Wildwood Lake, I was overwhelmed by the majesty of all the huge trees, and the homes that looked like small mansions...

One of my favorite times, though, was when there was a party or family gathering and Uncle George would sit down at the Steinway in the living room and play the songs he knew by heart. I don't know if he was a baritone or a bass. I only know that when he sang those deep tones, I felt the walls quiver. He played the songs that he'd danced to decades before with Bojangles (the same Bojangles from the Shirley Temple movies I adored). He sang "Summertime" from Porgy and Bess and classic gospel hymns like "Swing Low, Sweet Chariot." And then there was the Alma Mater...

George's passion and talent for music manifested in his Wabash College Glee Club, as well as the Mtn. Lakes Glee Club where he was a frequent soloist. Ted Milkey, the Glee Club's conductor, became a close friend and from the friendship the Alma Mater was born: the music by Ted Milkey and the lyrics by George, written while commuting on the train to New York City. The Mountain Lakes Alma Mater was premiered in the living room at 49 Briarcliff Rd., in 1950.

I'm naturally a bit biased in my love for this timeless song; it has an especially personal meaning. But I also know it is cherished by current and former residents of Mtn. Lakes. I've been heartened to know that for decades football coach Doug Wilkins had The Herd sing the alma mater at the end of every football game. It has been a unifying force with universal appeal... With the popularity of Facebook as a way for many "old Mountain Lakers" to reconnect—or connect for the first time through the common history of our childhood home, the words from the alma mater resonate more deeply than even before. It has been often said: Whether or not you currently live there – once a Laker, always a Laker.

Spring's Kaleidoscope

Spring comes to life with the first daffodil and hyacinth popping through a light blanket of snow. The robins return and with them a light heart. We leave our chilly homes, turn our faces to the sun, and prepare to enjoy the great outdoors in other familiar ways. Spring brings the first forays into the lakes and woods after the snow and ice melt. It is the time when we shiver in the sun trying to get the first tan of the season. Ice skating gives way to fishing and boating. We wrap up the season with reverence and remembrances at the solemn and exciting ceremonies—Memorial Day and Graduation Day, respectively—both marking new endings and new beginnings. And it is here we shed the shackles of school responsibilities and embrace the freedom of summer!

My Favorite Spring Memories
(What's in your spring kaleidoscope of Growing Up Laker?)

Summer

Chapter Four

Birchwood Lake.

On the *Growing Up Laker* calendar, summer started when school ended. Most of the time it was mid-June, but when the winter gods were their cruelest, we often found ourselves languishing until the end of June…without air conditioning…sticking to the classroom seats. We shed our shoes and were barefoot from Memorial Day to Labor Day. We gingerly walked in the grass, driveway, and streets, slowly building up calloused pads to get us through summer. As summer wore on our feet burned as we traversed the town hopping from grassy patch to shaded spot along the roads. Sometimes we'd try to walk on our beach towel. So often we wished we brought our shoes! Occasionally we'd take a rest from hopping along to keep from burning the soles of our feet to pop tar bubbles or swirl sticks in it to make tar babies. The graveled roads and beach parking lots presented other challenges. The gravel was more like shards of stone that cut into you like nobody's business. Then, by mid-summer the oil came.

Summer's heat and lack of rain resulted in dust clouds every time cars drove on the gravel roads and parking lots. To remedy this, the town sent trucks out to lay down a sheet of oil much to our parents'—mostly moms'—annoyance. We learned to come in the house through the back door, crawl upstairs to the bathroom so as not to soil the carpet. We scrubbed to remove the oil (and tar) from our feet, but no matter how hard we tried, stained feet were a summer reality. Likewise, stubbed toes and the road rash from turning the corner too quickly on our bicycles and wiping out were a summer bane.

We lived in our bathing suit: wake up, put on bathing suit, head to beach, swim and play all day, put clothes on over it to come to dinner, take off before bed (or maybe just sleep in it). After a few days the stench from lake water and sweat was overpowering, so we'd hop in the shower, soap up, and hang the suit up to dry. Next morning, we'd don that cold, damp suit and do it all again. Every now and then our mothers rescued those bathing suits and gave them a proper washing.

Summer was a time of dodging horseflies in the water and on the beach, outrunning deerflies along Birchwood trail, providing sustenance to mosquitos, and watching the lightning bugs magically appear as the sun set. Summer brings swimming, fishing, boating, biking, tennis, neighborhood games, and hanging out with friends—until we reach summer job age. It's a time of great adventures, flashlight tag, and swimming in every lake in town.

Neighborhood activities were the norm—cookouts with neighbors and ball games in the biggest yard in the neighborhood. We played in the woods and around the lakes all year round. We built campfires in the woods behind our houses, much to the dismay of neighborhood mothers who thought we'd burn the town down. Oh, the things we did at five, six, seven years of age! We made mud pies and tar babies, skimmed the algae off the lakes and made "soup." We adopted stray cats and ducks abandoned by their mothers. We held pageants, plays, and carnivals in our back yards. We created haunted houses complete with grape eyeballs and spaghetti brains. There was no end to our creativity.

We could always count on community activities to keep us busy too. Summer events and programs started with the Memorial Day Parade, crescendo-ed at 4th of July festivities and wrapped up with Labor Day celebration events. Couched between these were Hub Lakes League sponsored athletic events—swimming, diving, softball, and track. The borough also sponsored the Summer Recreation Program. The program employed teenagers as recreation counselors—often the first opportunity for kids to have a real summer job. I imagine that job was like herding cats from one activity to another. We played games in the gym and outside on the school grounds, did arts and crafts, and theoretically stayed out of trouble from nine till noon. I still can make a lanyard out of the flat plastic string. There were freckle contests, dance contests and myriad others spawned by the imagination of our recreation counselors. In fourth grade I was Twist Queen and Sam Stovall was the Twist King. Now there's something to crow about!

Boating, Swimming, and Fishing

Summer marked the emergence of four-legged canoes making their way down the street to the shores of the lakes. Kids pulling boat trailers and carrying sails were common sights as well. Boats transported us in ways our bikes could not. Sailboats, canoes, and rowboats filled the lakes as summer progressed. Rowboats seemed to lurk in the smaller waters, providing a more leisurely and stable ride for young and old alike. Sailing took some skill…and some luck with the wind. Wax the boat, carry the sail, assemble the boat, pile on your friends and hope the wind cooperates. On a breezy day, you could find yourself traversing the entire length and width of the Big Lake. And when the wind died…there you were stuck and vulnerable to attack by lake pirates wanting to tip you over. When the wind took a long siesta, you just had to jump in and pull your sailboat home to the other end of the lake.

Growing Up Laker

Dam along Wildwood Lake (top). Traveling the Canal (bottom).

Canoes on the other hand relied solely on kid power. They could easily navigate the shallow passage through the Canal, expanding our watery explorations from Wildwood Lake to Mountain Lake. It took some effort though to traverse the Big Lake in a canoe. And when we stopped to rest, we were just as vulnerable to attack by the lake

Summer

pirates as the sailboats and a bit more difficult to right once tipped. Underneath a capsized canoe, however, was another world—hidden from view, our secrets echoed, oxygen grew thin, and the realization that we'd eventually have to right this beast emerged.

Our earliest childhood swimming memories include chilly, early morning swim lessons at Island Beach from lifeguards trying to make an extra dollar or two. Passing our swim test was another rite of passage. At the start of every season, we swim to the far rope, swim half way back, tread water for one minute, come back to shore when the life guard blows the whistle, and get our beach tag painted (nail polish on the metal badges; marker on the newer plastic ones).

Collection of beach tags on display at the Mountain Lakes Library.

Summer also meant mother-mandated swim team workouts at Birchwood Beach and ensuing Hub Lakes and Lakeland swim meets on Monday and Wednesday nights respectively (Never tell your mother "I'm bored" at the start of the summer!). We lounge around on towels in sweatpants and sweatshirts waiting for our race. We plug our ears with lamb's wool and don our white swim caps. We consume boxes of dry Jell-O and play cards to pass the time between rooting for our teammates. And who can forget the traditional post-meet trip to Denville for Dairy Queen? Long lines at the double service windows, iconic swirl at the top of the cone. Chocolate or red hard shell dipped cones, hot fudge sundaes, strawberry sundaes, banana splits, dilly bars, and more all accompanied by thin wisps of napkins that didn't do a darn thing to stem or capture the flow of melting ice cream on a hot summer night.

Beach days are filled with playing Marco Polo, diving for popsicle sticks, practicing flips off the docks, having chicken fights (one person perched on the shoulders of another would try to knock the other pair over). We play card games, including the one that left our knuckles bruised and bloody, and listen to our AM/FM radios. We get in trouble for hanging on the ropes, pushing others in, and sundry other infractions that result in sitting out or picking up cigarette butts. Imagine that punishment today!

Midvale Boat Dock with Island Beach in the background (top).
Island Beach with the Club in the background (bottom).

When we aren't swimming at the official beaches, we're dropping into Crystal Lake from the Mueser's rope swing or swinging from vines along the shores. We swim from our docks or the neighbors' docks without having to follow any lifeguard rules. On a brave and daring day, we swim from the Club or Midvale Boat Dock to Island Beach. We have to be a bit sneakier when departing Island Beach…ducking between boats docked at the end of the beach and ignoring the whistles and shouts of the lifeguards. The trip between the Midvale Boat Dock and Island Beach is a convenient short cut for kids on a mission. Steve McCurdy ('72) tells of his lunchtime delivery service.

My brother was a lifeguard at Island Beach and my mother would often give me his lunch in a paper sack and a towel and tell me to swim across the lake to take him his lunch. I swam backstroke and developed a pretty strong kick which helped me out on summer swim teams at Birchwood and later in high school.[3]

Sundays at church were bookended by early morning boat races on the Big Lake and afternoon swim races at Birchwood Lake. Nature's bounty in Mountain Lakes had a way of providing spiritual sustenance that complemented that which we received in our churches. We had early morning sailing races that filled the Big Lake with color. I could look out my third-floor window and spy the boats on the lake across the Boulevard. Sunday afternoons were spent at Birchwood Beach participating in or watching the handicap swim races. Remember the point system, the handicap time delays, and the winnings posted on the beach bulletin board?

When the sun went down, the suits came off—it was skinny dipping time! *Growing Up Laker* was all about heading to the lakes at night with friends, having a few beers, stripping down and diving in... and hoping no one stole your clothes or shined the headlights on you!

Fishing was another aspect of *Growing Up Laker*. While I didn't share my father's or my brother Lee's passion for fishing, I did go fishing *once* with my father on Crystal Lake. I had a yellow and black fishing rod. We were in a canoe and I caught a bass and a pickerel. That's all I remember. I went to the Trout Derby each spring and caught sunnies across the street in Shadow Lake a time or two. The fishing fever never took hold. But for those who discovered the joy of fishing, Mountain Lakes was the place to be. Nine lakes or ponds, all with sweet spots. There were secluded spots along the shores of every lake. If you were lucky to live on the lake, you could fish right from your yard or dock. If you had a boat, you could hop in and head to the middle of the lake or to that hard-to-reach place from shore. There were all types of fish—bass, catfish, crappies, perch, pickerel, sunnies—and the occasional muskrat, water moccasin, and snapping turtle. Parents (usually fathers) passed on their fishing skills and secrets to children: where to fish, when to fish, bait to use, etc.

Summer

Our fathers Thomas Stewart ('43) and James Barnes ('51) on the lakes.

Kids who fished tended to lose track of time. My father Jim Barnes lived at 105 Kenilworth Road. *"My father had a garden—one shovelful brought enough worms to fish Wildwood dam. When my mother wanted me, she would beep the car horn three times."*

Snippets of his childhood fish tales include

bass in Wildwood, pickerel in Sunset, catfish in Crystal, and a 50-lb catfish in Shadow Carl Hazel hooked…he had it on for hours. It towed him and his boat from Shadow to Olive Lake where I tried to throw it onto the beach. I won a fishing contest with a 23-inch pickerel caught under a willow tree next to the Club with a jitterbug hung on a limb and Bobby Wilson won with a five-lb bass.

We'll pause here so you can share your own fish tales.

Hiking and Biking

As our feet recall, we walked *everywhere*. Sometimes we rode bikes, but walking was the preferred method of transportation. We explored paths through the woods, around Birchwood Lake. We often walked down the Boulevard, past the Tourne, along Powerville Road, down around old Denville Road, Norris Road and up Pocono Road. We walked along the railroad tracks. We cut through yards to reach our destinations. Our trekking adventures took most of the day, but what else was there to do? When we tired of walking, we hopped on our bikes.

We rode our bikes to Denville to the Viking Bakery and over by Indian Lake to the penny candy store. The ride there was dangerously downhill, the ride back was more of a push-the-bike uphill ordeal. We rode to Del's Village and the Market, which was a bit less arduous, depending on where you lived. We rode to the beach, we tried to ride through the woods, and we rode to our friends' houses. We rode just to feel a little breeze on a sweltering day. And quite often our dog would be trailing behind! Riding our bikes—bikes of all sorts—graduating from bikes with no gears/coaster brakes to three-speed models with hand brake options, banana seat bikes, and ultimately on to the five-gear and ten-gear "racing" bikes with curved handlebars! We pulled wagons and skateboarders behind us. We rode solo, but most often we travelled with someone perched on the handlebars, the crossbar of a boy's bike, or astride the back fender. Skilled cyclists might even try transporting more than one friend!

At some point during our walking or biking, we abandoned the asphalt and ventured into the woods. Whether it was to beat the heat or take a shortcut to another location, the woods were a welcome diversion. We could climb trees and large rocks, splash in spring fed brooks, shoot at the rifle range, or simply explore. The woods held abandoned foundations, our camp sites, tree forts, hidden stashes, and our secrets. They contained poison ivy, felled trees, moss covered rocks, and jack-in-the-pulpit plants. Deer, snakes, skunks, raccoons, birds, and who knows what else we didn't see shared the woods with us. And it always amazed this navigationally and geographically challenged girl that we could start at one end of town (Birchwood), walk through some woods, and end up at the opposite end of town (the Tourne). The woods surrounded us and were so much a part of us, that we couldn't imagine a place without them.

Summer Jobs

Growing up in a small town like Mountain Lakes required a certain amount of creativity when it came to earning money. Perusing the HPC Laker Profiles and the Growing Up Laker surveys provide a glimpse into the entrepreneurial spirit of Laker kids. On the younger side of money-making, we held carnivals and talent shows. We had lemonade stands all around town. We did chores for our parents and neighbors. We collected soda bottles to return for deposits (remember the days before plastic?). When we got older, we mowed lawns, painted houses, repaired docks on the lake, cleaned houses, had paper routes, baby sat, served at our parents' parties. Frank Wiswall (b. 1919) made one penny for pulling ten weeds; in late 1960s we got a penny per dandelion (or was it two?), but it had to include the root. Jack Lee (b. ca 1910) recalled making money delivering mail in town.[1] Delivering magazines and the mail, raising/selling eggs, making lead soldiers,

and raising/selling plants were also popular means for making a few dollars in the early years of Mountain Lakes (Jack Lee, Ralph Wells, David Higgins).[1] Albert Earle worked at the Club. *"The tennis courts were clay. I had to line them every morning and the lime would clog the lining machine and I had to put my arm in the tub up to my elbow to unplug it. I also worked at the Club as a pinsetter. The duck pins would fly away and there was not much room to hide."*[1] And in later decades, we were employed by the town as lifeguards, snack shack attendants, summer recreation counselors, sports coaches, and tennis tag checkers. We worked at local restaurants, delicatessens, gas stations, grocery stores, factories and manufacturing plants, department stores, country clubs, hospitals, nursing homes, hotels, the YMCA, feed mills and horse stables. Our parents put us to work at their businesses.

One of our favorite entrepreneurial ventures from the *Growing Up Laker* survey is from Pam Shaw Burzynski ('74):

One summer my brothers and I spent on what we preferred to call "Shaw's Pond," turtle hunting....We decided instead of selling lemonade (how boring) or something lame like that we thought we might be able to turn a buck selling turtles. There were loads of turtles in Shaw's Pond, so all we had to do was catch them and figure out the boys from the girls, pair them up and then we'd be in the turtle breeding business. We devised a pretty good plan for catching "painted" turtles....We'd sneak up as close as we could (taking turns rowing and netting) to the turtles sleeping on the rocks. The plan was to get as close to them as possible so that when they saw us and jumped off the rocks into the water we'd be within striking distance of being able to scoop them up in the net while they tried to swim away....At one point we had about seven or eight turtles in our basement...in these big metal bins that we tried to simulate the lake conditions, in the hope that we would end up with lots of little turtles. One of our turtles was a three-legged turtle, named Pepe. We were pretty sure a fish or a snapping turtle had eaten his one leg. Pepe was our favorite. Our basement got pretty smelly that summer, and we didn't have any luck producing turtle offspring, so eventually, we released all the turtles back into the lake and gave up the thoughts of breeding turtles.[3]

Spontaneous Fun

There was more to summer fun *Growing Up Laker* than swimming, boating, fishing, hiking and biking. We attended summer camp. We spent the day on the tennis courts at the Club, Park Lakes Tennis Club, or at the high school. We played Little League baseball, pick-up games of basketball and baseball, and street hockey in our neighborhoods, at community courts, and school yards. We visited the library and hung out at friends' houses. We formed bands and played music in our basements, third floors, garages and carriage houses. We played games with the neighborhood gang—cowboys, war, hide-n-seek, croquet, kickball, softball, wiffleball, tag, kick the can, flashlight tag. Somehow, we squeezed all this in between the Independence Day and Labor Day.

Independence Day

Independence Day—the Fourth of July—meant all day sports events around town along with races and celebrations at the Mountain Lakes Club—a time when everyone was welcome. *"The mayor, George Rose, would come out to the end of the catwalk in his lemon yellow linen pants, white bucks and tan linen jacket to start the festivities"* (Gale Lester Butler, '64).[1] The day's events began early with the traditional canoe and sailboat races. There was the Island Beach Swim starting at Island Beach and ending at the Club. And don't forget the greased watermelon contest where kids risked their lives to cling to a silly oversized fruit! The kickboard and swim races ensued—different age groups for boys and girls. In the early days, races took place in the Big Lake at the Club, then later in the Club pool. Beyond the lake and the Club were Old Timers softball games at Briarcliff, tennis games, and who knows what else. Finally, there were trophies, ribbons, and a host of accolades for all participants. All these activities culminated with the best lakeside picnics and fireworks display we could ever imagine.

View of Mountain Lakes Club from Island Beach.

Since the early days of Mountain Lakes, kids were having fun on the 4th of July. There were parent-vs-kids softball games on Neafie's Field and neighborhood fireworks displays. Long before fireworks on the Big Lake, Ralph Wells (b. 1916) recalled Mr. Edris bringing home a carload of fireworks and setting them off in the neighborhood in the empty lot next door. When the town took over the fireworks display, folks took to the lakes to watch the show. Some paddled their canoes from Wildwood Lake through the Canal to the Big Lake. Faith Witham Robertson remembers: *"When the fireworks went off you could feel the canoe vibrate from the explosions and see the lights coming at you and it would be so exciting."*[1] The yards along the lake were lined with flares from Fusee Flare Factory and every kid in town had sparklers to light up their little slice of the night. During the blackout times of World War II, Carolyn Carlson Mills recalled Fourth of July fireworks consisting of the fire department shooting water up into the air and shining colored light on it.[1]

Before the Club built the swimming pool, families that didn't live on the lake or visit those who did, gathered on the beach and lawn

at the Club to watch the fireworks. We parked at Lake Drive School or along the street, walked behind the Club, spread our blankets on the ground, and waited for the show to begin. When we got older, we paddled or rowed out to the middle of the lake, plopped down in the bottom of the boat, and enjoyed the show. We didn't need radio music synched with the display—the oohs and ahs were enough.

Labor Day

Labor Day weekend signals the end of summer for kids Growing Up Laker. Swimming championships are over. Summer jobs are winding down. The beaches are empty as families squeeze in their last vacation of the season. Parents start back-to-school preparations—clothes and school supply shopping. And at this tail end of summer are the Labor Day celebrations bringing more of the same events as the 4th of July. Boat races, swim races, and other athletic events. Trophies and ribbons. Too much sun. There's just something comforting in the familiar rhythm and routine of community events.

Summer's Kaleidoscope

Growing Up Laker in summertime is like living in our very own adventure park or favorite story book. We play every imaginable game, have myriad venues and toys at our disposal. We spend three months being hot, sweaty, and sunburned and wouldn't have it any other way. We seek refuge from the heat in the waters and woods. We smell of lake water, baby oil, zinc oxide, worms, and campfires. Reflections of the sails of boats dance on the water. They are most beautiful from a third story window.

The beach sand is cold to the feet in the early morning hours. Lifeguards rake the sand. The water laps at the shore; there's a gentle breeze. A few fishing-souls dot the lakes. Soon the beaches and lakes will fill with swimmers, boaters, and sunbathers. The fish will head to deeper, shadier spots. As for me, well, it's the end of August. The dragonflies are back and fly around me as I sit in the neighbor's rowboat on Shadow Lake. We've come full circle. Welcome back fall!

My Favorite Summer Memories
(What's in your summer kaleidoscope of Growing Up Laker?)

Part II

The Spirit of Place

The magic of Mountain Lakes lies in its places—the woods, the hills, the lakes, the homes and other dwelling spaces. *Growing Up Laker*, we all had special places that called to us. They sparked our imaginations, sheltered us, revived our spirit. They served as meeting places, hangouts, campsites, and places to free our adventurous souls. Here we explore the spirit of these special Laker places. We trek deep into the woods, traverse the hills, wade into the waters, and finally rest a spell in those favorite dwelling places we claim as our own.

Our Mountains
Chapter Five

Looking downhill on Martin's Lane (top).
Sled Run path between Tower Hill Road and Overlook Road (bottom).

Hapgood and Van Duyne had good reason to call our borough Mountain Lakes. We had big hills—mountains—all around us. Well, perhaps not Adirondack- or Catskill-sized mountains, but monumental hills, nonetheless. They seemed like mountains to us kids, having little world perspective. They gave us climbing and riding challenges and places to sled. We walked and pushed our bikes uphill, leaning forward till our knees and noses almost scraped the road. We prayed the brakes would hold as we flew down on those bikes. We hoped we could detour into yards or roll off our sleds before cars crossed our paths. And in our teen years we navigated those steep roads in our cars.

Atop those mountains stood the water tower—to climb and watch the sunrise, to paint our graduation year on, or to take the ultimate dare and dive in for a swim (Susan Bruton Bailey Cole, '57).[4] And maybe, just maybe, it became the world's largest gong. *"There was a water tower being constructed up on Tower Hill. Somebody had the bright idea of going up there and throwing some rocks at it...There must have been 20 of us. That thing, you could have heard it resonating all the way to Dover. It was horrendous"* (Tom Brackin, '53).[1]

There were BIG houses up on those mountains—even the street names evoked a loftiness—Tower Hill, Lookout, Crestview. From those homes—the porches, the balconies or the third floor windows—we could look out beyond the Big Lake, beyond the Village, beyond fields and woods all the way to the horizon. And at night the view transformed from pastoral beauty to a magnificent lightscape of New York City. These views reminded us that we lived in a perfect place nestled between a woodland paradise and the bustle of arts and opportunity.

The mountains were ideal for winter sport. We flew down North Glen, Briarcliff, Ball, Hillcrest, Crystal and Pollard Roads and every hill and yard in between during the heavy snows. The most popular and talked about sledding sites in the 1920s and 1930s were North Glen and Pollard Roads. Traffic back then was light and slow; however, there were times when borough officials closed the streets so kids and parents alike to enjoy the ride. In time our sledding venues expanded to include the hills behind Saint Clare's Hospital and the Tower Hill sled run.

The Tower Hill sled run was an attempt to create an official safe venue for sledding. Located on an early undeveloped road between Tower Hill and Overlook Roads, it was a 1,500-foot trail that started at the access path from Tower Hill and steadily descended to Overlook Road. It was a local venue like most sledding hills and for years we had it to ourselves before the borough installed flood lights in the mid-to late 1960s. Even then, it wasn't used by many except neighborhood kids. The main roads and backyard trails continued to be the sled runs of choice.

Now these hills weren't just for sledding and flying down on our bikes. They served a vital function during the days of gas rationing during WWII. Amy's father, Tom Stewart ('43) told her that during gas

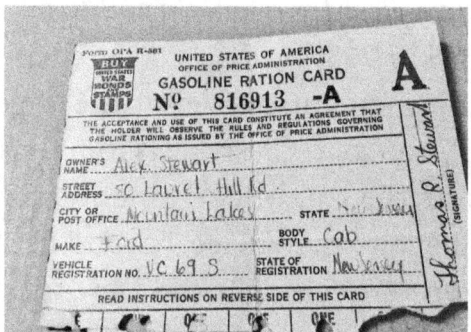
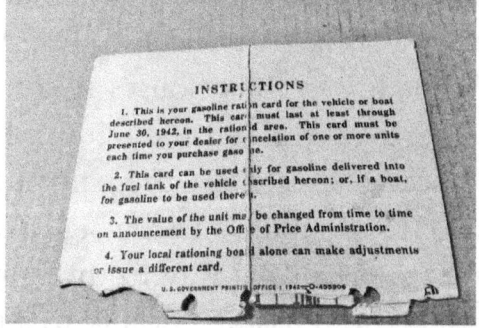

1942 gas rationing card.

rationing, they would turn off the engines and coast down the hills to save gas. I wonder if any of us turned off the engines and coasted down the hills to save fuel during the gas shortages and odd-even gas rationing of 1973 and 1979?

When the snows melted, our forays into the hills changed focus. We traded our sleds for bikes, but mountains being mountains, it was easier just to hoof it. We traversed the hills of our town to get to school, friends' houses, and to take shortcuts from one hangout to another. The most iconic of these mountain trails is the one from Birchwood to the Tourne. And our talk of mountains would not be complete without a visit to the Tourne.

The Tourne, magic words! What small boy or old boy has ever lived within walking distance of the strange mountain...and now sees the name in print, will not stop and think in retrospect the happy hours he has spent on this elevation. Should he now be an old boy...and far removed from the place of his childhood, what thoughts the name must conjure up, and what memories of the good old days will cause his heart to pulsate to a quicker beat. (Willis 1924, 31)

According to Mrs. Jean Ricker, former Boonton Township Historian, recorded history of the Tourne began when

John Chapman surveyed and returned a 1,507 acre tract to James Bollen....The tract stretched northward toward Rockaway Valley.... It must be noted here that no member of the 1715 expedition was impressed by the craggy prospect on 'the Other side' of the great Rocky Hill, that expanse of primeval forest which would, in the future, embrace all of Boonton, and parts of Boonton Township, Taylortown, and Mountain Lakes.[2]

Mrs. Ricker wonders whether this survey crew "*cut bridle paths over the narrow footways made by tawny inhabitants of the nearby plantation? Did a Lenape guide point out the two remarkable mountain springs where thirsty man and nickering horse might find refreshment?*"[2]

The Tourne property was handed down throughout the years and landed in the hands of Clarence Addington DeCamp, who in the late 1800s transformed the area into the Tourne we know today. "*Using only shovel, axe, pick and crow bar [sic], he built single-handedly a road to the 'Top of the Tourne' and cleared paths which are still used today. Everyone was welcome on his beloved mountain.*"[2] Today, the keepers of the Tourne continue DeCamp's vision of welcoming visitors to this beautiful place.

In an effort to expand his treasure and protect its access, DeCamp purchased the Rattlesnake Meadow reservation, 94 acres of swamp and sprout land in May 1891. This area continues to be known by its original name *"and is testimony to the fact that native sons and daughters have cherished and preserved the names under which our localities were born."*[2] More details may be found in *The History of The Tourne*, located on the Mountain Lakes official website's Historical Essays page.

When all other forms of amusement have failed the small boys of the neighborhood, "Let's go up on the Tourne!" has always been a mandate which quickened them to new activities. Then, after a long climb the summit being reached, there was nothing to do except lie or sit down, gaze out over the country and drink in the ozone from the air. (Willis 1924, 31-32)

We hiked to the Tourne and around the Tourne with friends and families. Saturday and Sundays were often family picnic days at the Tourne. We played ball and ran around. Some even rode horses there.

We used to go horseback riding too all up through the Tourne where they still had all of the roads from the ice-cutting days. You could babysit for 25 cents an hour… for four hours, and then you could horseback ride for an hour. (Myrtle Hillman Kingsley)[1]

Kids born in the 1940s recall reading *Scouts of '76* by Charles Willis and retracing the same trails and discovering stone walls. The *Scouts of '76* brought local history to life for young readers and fueled a lifelong passion for history for some. The Tourne, surrounded by woodlands was just one of many destinations and hangouts for kids *Growing Up Laker.*

Our mountains and our woods are inextricably connected. How do we reminisce about the hills without talking of the woods? Let's venture into the woods and discover their allure.

My Favorite Mountain Dwelling Places
(What's in your kaleidoscope of Growing Up Laker?)

Our Woods
Chapter Six

As previously mentioned, *Scouts of '76: A Tale of the Revolutionary War* by Charles E. Willis was a popular, albeit mandatory, read in the 1950s for kids *Growing Up Laker*. The stories were set in the areas surrounding Mountain Lakes. In his foreword he writes:

> *Why invent localities for a narrative when there are real ones to be used? ...The localities are as described and will be readily recognized by many a boy as well as boys grown up. They were the hunting, fishing, and play grounds [sic] of the writer in his youthful days.*

(The book is dedicated to the Boy Scouts of America; hence, the emphasis on boys). Reading the book reminds us of the connection we had to these woods as children, just like the children in these tales—Russel and Serpent, his Lenni Lenape friend.

Thanks to the vision of Lewis Van Duyne, Herbert Hapgood and other early settlers of Mountain Lakes Residential Park, the woodlands were an integral part of our lives. Originally a *"rural woodland owned by a few families,"* Lewis Van Duyne set his sights on developing *"a large tract of pristine land, one of rolling hills, woods, swamps and boulders located along the city-bound branch of the Lackawanna Railroad"* (History of Mountain Lakes).

Although the developers cleared the land to construct the homes, native trees and plants returned to claim their place. Additionally, two major events contributed to the preservation of our wooded playground: the 1938 acquisition of titles to many of the undeveloped building lots in the borough and the 1952 purchase of 250 acres of woodland around Crystal and Birchwood Lakes and up to the Tourne. These preservation efforts are what made our woodland adventures possible *Growing Up Laker*. In these wooded areas between Birchwood and the Tourne we discover two other historical sites visited by kids over the decades—Rattlesnake Meadow and the Spring House.

In the early days, Rattlesnake Meadow, aka Rattlesnake Valley was indeed a snake infested, swampy valley turned farmland. *"Miles of laboriously constructed walls, springs and water holes, foundations, and ditches attest to the work put in by early settlers to earn a livelihood from the land."*[2] Since the founding of Mountain Lakes, it has been a popular hiking trail *"now mostly a narrow path although its earlier width is clearly discernible."*[2] This snake infested woodland held the popular Hound and Hare Race for 8th grade graduates of the 1920s and 1930s. School officials orchestrated a graduation celebration with a

> *Hare and Hound chase through the woods and along Rattlesnake Valley. A dozen or so "hares" would be set loose with half an hour head start and the obligation to drop bits of paper along the route they followed. They were followed by the rest of the class, the "hounds," who chased them to a destination. Sometimes this was the "Bubbling Spring." (A lovely little spring dug and lined with stones centuries ago. It has not run dry in the last 60 years).* (Roland Mueser)[2]

Is it possible that this bubbling spring may be close to the Spring House—another historical woodland landmark?

The Spring House is located along the trail that leaves the Tourne and heads toward Birchwood Lake. According to the instructions in the historical essay, about a half-mile up the trail, there is an intersection with a blue blazed trail. Turn left on this trail, cross two creeks, follow the trail to the right and up the hill. The Spring House is about 60 feet off to the left in the woods. *"This stone foundation back in the woods once supported a small shed. A spring bubbles up inside it, flows through an opening in the stone and forms a stream that runs away down hill* [sic]."[2] Amy and I attempted to find the Spring House in the summer of 2019 without any luck (as you recall, I confessed to being navigationally and geographically challenged). Despite our best efforts and those of our husbands we couldn't even find the blue blazed trail. Perhaps others will.

Although the history of the Spring House is not clear it seems to have been built to collect drinking water. Some believe it was built by the farming residents of the 18th and 19th centuries. Some think Hapgood may have built it to augment water from residents' wells. Once its original purpose expired however, the Spring House became a smoking hangout for local teens during the 1920s and 1930s. Eventually the Spring House faded into the landscape and its story forgotten.

Our Playing Grounds

Long before there were *Into the Woods* and *Where the Wild Things Are*, kids were fueling their own imaginations and creating their own adventurous worlds. And so it was *Growing Up Laker*. We were surrounded by woods. If they didn't border our back or side yards, they were across the street or short jog away. Fallen trees from past ice storms were transformed in our world of make-believe. Upon these downed trees we walked the plank of our pirate ship, we traversed the high wire of our circus, and we patrolled the parapet of our castle. We stored our treasures in the hollow spaces. The springs and tiny brooks quenched our thirst. The wet clay that formed the basin and banks of these water spots made for building blocks and ammunition, or dishes and furniture for the faeries and woodland spirits.

We built our cabins, forts, and clubhouses in those woods from branches and rocks, supplemented by items from our garages, basements, and backyard sheds. These were our playhouses, our camp bases, our hideouts, and our blood-brother, secret password clubhouses.

David Higgins and Skip Watts remember wonderful cabins. David (b. 1922) notes

> *[In] the woods, which is now Richard Wilcox Park near the Tourne, there used to be several log cabins, built by young fellows who lived in Mountain Lakes. When you think of it, just hand tools, no power tools. This was the twenties, early thirties. I remember two log cabins, specifically. One was in what was called Rattlesnake Swamp…Adams*

cabin. There was another one on the hill going down into Rattlesnake Swamp, on the side of the hill about a quarter of a mile away...built by a fellow by the name of Shute and his friends. When you think back, it was quite an undertaking. It had a second floor that overhung the first floor—all out of logs. There was a fireplace and chimney— stones mortared in. Open windows. A dirt floor downstairs, a wood floor on the second floor. A roof with planks and tarpaper on it. It was probably a good half-mile down this hill. Little narrow path. Sandbags of cement and stones for the fireplace and chimney were hauled in and water from a nearby stream. The last time I was at the big one—it had purposely been torn down. That was in 1942. It was sad to see it go.[1]

Skip Watts ('44) recalls

There was a family named Hobby who lived on Morris Avenue. And the Hobby boys were absolutely the world's greatest log cabin builders going. And they had...at least four log cabins built out in Rattlesnake Meadow. There was the block house at Bubbling Springs. There was the log cabin at Deer Ridge and there were a couple of others out there. And I can remember as a kid, oh, my Lord, every summer I would disappear, and I'd spend the summer out living in one of those log cabins.[1]

Forts were springing up in other woods as well...Kenilworth Road, all along Powerville Road, in the woods around the Upper Lakes of Birchwood and Crystal, and in the woods of the Village.

Constance and Faith Witham (b. 1919/1922) lived on the corner of Kenilworth and Powerville Roads and shared their woodland story:

Woods. Just woods (where Wildwood School and football field are now). And all woods down Powerville. That's where we used to play, in the woods. We didn't worry about being girls. We could be pirates or explorers. One of the amazing things was that my brother and Henry Barton, who lived on Briarcliff, I think, south of Wildwood Lake, they went into the woods west of Powerville Road and they put ropes on a very tall tree in a clearing. They were being Tarzans. And they also built platforms on trees at the edge of the clearing. They'd get a sympathetic swing going with the rope and it would go flying up and wrap around one of the branches that they had put in place to form the platform. And then you'd climb up the tree. Get on the rope. There was a knot on the bottom of the rope, and you'd swing down, back and forth across the clearing.[1]

Thirty years later in the woods between Kenilworth Road and the High School, we played and leapt over the small brook that ran through there. We built campfires much to the dismay of one neighborhood mother. Thinking we'd burn the woods down, she chastised us and threatened to call the fire department.

In the Village, when Woodland Avenue was a dead-end street, *"we had acres of woods in which to play cowboys, soldiers, or build forts...There were many other boys...and together we had some very organized 'wars' and built some very sophisticated tree forts and underground structures"* (Robert H. Braunohler, '64).[1] Another popular woodland playground was north of the Grove Place turnaround.

Nestled in the woods throughout the town we discovered foundations of homes never realized. John Jack Lee (arr. ML 1918) recalls "rattling around" in Hapgood homes that were never completed.

There was big sport for the kids to go in those homes and play hide-go-seek and climb around them...the walls were not yet plastered... And we would kick out the lathe [sic] so we had ladders and you could climb all over the houses. And there were lots of nooks and crannies to hide.[1]

There were two abandoned house foundations along the Sled Run between Tower Hill Road and Overlook Road that I liked to explore. According to old town maps, they were built along roads envisioned by Hapgood, but never realized. They were my very own fortresses.

House foundation along the Sled Run.

Our Hunting Grounds

In the early days of the town, the woods provided hunting grounds for residents—for sport, income, or sustenance. Hunters travelled along the roads and the wooded trails to hunt for a variety of animals. According to the Rifle Range historical essay, the original shooting range used for target practice by local enthusiasts and by the police was a sand pit just south of Route 46 (it was called Bloomfield Avenue at that time). My father, James Barnes notes that

> *during WWII my father was an air raid warden. We would walk through the woods toward Fanny Road and the range was just behind the little league field. We would shoot toward Powerville Road into a big bank. Before that the police would shoot under the "Sweet Shop" down by the railway tracks, next to the jail.*

After World War II, interest in hunting and fishing continued and the Mountain Lakes Rod and Gun Club was formed. Members went deep in the woods behind Mountain Lakes for target practice and competition. This rifle range was located beyond the cul-de-sac of Crystal Road (which was not built until the early to mid-1960s). Dennis Waldron ('66) says *"My dad built two NRA rifle ranges, as he was a qualified instructor – one in the Tourne prior to it becoming a park. The park service did not allow it to continue. A second range was constructed near Birchwood Lake and Crystal Lake. The railroad tie backstop still mostly exists."*[1] The site was almost impenetrable and the trek to it quite arduous. Those who used the rifle range improved it by constructing a backstop of heavy railroad ties that were carried uphill from the Birchwood Lake area. Kids would come from all over town and trek through the woods to the rifle range. They'd sling their .22 rifles across their shoulders, and no one would say a word. Imagine carrying a rifle down the street today! The Boy Scouts also used the rifle range and surrounding woods to hone their survival skills. It was in these woods, they receive gun training and safety lessons, learned the fine art of camping and worked on earning their badges.

By the 1970s, the rifle range was on its way out. Shooting was less popular, neighbors were complaining, scouting was on the decline, and Mountain Lakes was becoming more suburban. The focus of the Rod and Gun Club turned to fishing and maintaining the lakes; the club disbanded in the early 1980s. The rifle range—a popular spot for aficionados of all ages—was all but abandoned. The final chapter in the history of the rifle range was in 1987, when the Mountain Lakes Borough Council passed an ordinance forbidding the discharge of firearms within town limits.

Our Shortcuts

The woods provided both a vast playground and the backdrop for many a shortcut from one location to another. One of the most iconic shortcuts through the woods was "the Path" between Briarcliff School and the high school. The Path winds down a long hill, through the trees, and across a stream. It had a few side trails leading to our houses and a short passageway to the football field. It is the path for every student who travelled uphill to Briarcliff or downhill to the high school. It was the final leg of our two-mile walk to school. And it was the site of many bicycle crashes, teenage crushes, secret stashes, and clandestine smokes. We rehashed the weekend's antics, planned our next adventure, fretted about upcoming exams, and solved our monumental teen-age dilemmas. David Higgins recalls a special memory:

> *There's one place, I don't know whether I could find it. Behind Briarcliff School, in the woods there, heading down to the football field, my wife and I walked down there. Probably June of '42. There was a great big oak tree on which I carved our initials. I don't know*

Center: Blvd to Overlook, Top 2: Crystal Lake Path,
Bottom: Tower Hill to Tourne and railroad tracks.

whether it's still there or not. My initials DH and her initials MSL, Margaret Stanfield Lodge. With a pocket penknife. I was 20. She was 18. That was the year she graduated from high school.[1]

Oh, if that path could talk!

Shortcuts through the town were neighborhood specific—each travelled by local kids. Every street corner had at least one yard with a worn path across it. One of my favorite shortcuts was between the Boulevard and Overlook Road. A large puddingstone marked the entrance on the Boulevard, and the path led to an opening on Overlook Road across the street from the Leef's house. We could diverge from the path, cross our small campsite on the rise, and wind up in our side yard. We also hiked the sled run that took us from Tower Hill to Overlook Road and back again. And who can forget the rooted and rutted path between

Crystal Lake and Sunset Lake? Every kid who swam at Birchwood journeyed along this trail by foot or bike. It also doubled as a place for fishing, launching boats, nighttime skinny-dipping, and stolen kisses.

From the top of the town there were trails to the Tourne and to Birchwood. Several paths from Powerville Road and adjoining streets led to the Little League fields and the YMCA on Fanny Road. These paths diverged and t-boned into others that took us to destinations in every direction (David Lampp, '73).[4] Faith Witham Robertson (b. 1922) recalled the horse drawn garbage truck driving down the dead end of Kenilworth Road and into the woods. Perhaps kids traveling along paths in those woods came across the landfills long grown over with other vegetation. David Lampp recalls the trail behind his house on Melrose Road *"stopped on top of what appeared to be an old landfill with crabapple trees."*[4] These woods also held many small swampy areas and ponds that could be explored during summer and put to good use during winter. David recalls another trail that *"led past a small pond like area that would flood in the wintertime and freeze. I kept the ice free of sticks and limbs and was able to skate on it in the winter."*[4]

Down along the railroad tracks, kids followed paths that either paralleled them or led to them from Morris Avenue or Pollard Road. They dared each other to climb through the culverts that ran under the tracks.[1] Eric Russell remembers a path near the Market they dubbed "the cliffs" that ran above the railroad tracks *"from the basketball court behind Schultz's garage...to Pollard Rd. At the end there was a concrete tunnel carrying a little stream to cross under the tracks near Rockaway Terrace. Lots of frogs and salamanders."*[4]

Close by were paths that traversed Diaper Village and Yorke Village. These well-worn paths provided walking and bike riding shortcuts.[4] All throughout the woods in Mountain Lakes were trails that led to open spaces, small creeks and swampy areas that made for summer slogging and sloshing and winter skating.

So, what happens when a group of four-year-olds takes off without the knowledge of our coveted shortcuts? They venture out down the main roads. Here is the story of three kids on a quest for better cookies.

My brother Bob and his friends Mark and Jamie are playing at our house while their mothers did what mothers did back then…chat and drink coffee with half an eye trained on the kids. The boys decide that there are better cookies at Mark's house down off North Pocono Road, so off they set with tricycle and dog Toby in tow. Traversing down the Boulevard from Overlook Road to North Pocono, then along the narrow grassy path to their cookie destination, they arrive at Mark's house. Finally noticing the boys are nowhere to be found, the mothers call the police to search. Somehow, they figure out they must have made their way to Mark's house. Yep, there they were. Who knew in 1966 that three boys, a dog, and a trike could make it that far on a busy road such as North Pocono? Perhaps only in Mountain Lakes.

Whatever our game or pleasure—pioneers, pirates, soldiers, world explorers, scientists, spin-the-bottle, climbing trees, catching frogs, hopping rocks in the streams—the woods were home to wonderful thoroughfares and meeting places for kids of all ages. We grew up in those woods, honed our survival skills, and developed a sincere appreciation for nature's gifts.

My Favorite Wooded Dwelling Places
(What's in your kaleidoscope of Growing Up Laker?)

Our Lakes and Beaches

Chapter Seven

On the water, in the water, along its sacred shores, we learn many lessons. On the water, we learn to ride the winds from one end to another. We practice stillness and patience while awaiting a wind to carry us. When all else fails, we learn to use our own energy to propel us to shore. In the water, we learn about cycle of the seasons, the cycle of life, nature's dangers (water moccasins and snapping turtles), teamwork, competition, and the joys of simple play. Along the shores, we embark on adventures that turn into campfire tales about the one that got away. The shores give us resting spots for contemplation and quiet conversations. It's here the wind whispers to us through the language of leaves on dancing branches. The early morning sun invites us to explore the waters, the setting sun reminds us of the pleasures and peace the waters offer.

The Building of Our Lakes

Our town boasts many lakes; however, their origins stem from swampy, wooded valleys. According to Roland Mueser's historical essay, the three upper lakes—Crystal, Sunset, and Birchwood—were originally called Fox Hill Lakes and built to meet the growing demands for ice in the late 19th century. Ice was cut from the lakes into huge blocks, packed in thick blankets of sawdust and stored in ice houses until they were shipped out by rail to homes and businesses across New Jersey and New York City. The Fox Hills Ice Company acquired the tract of land north of Pocono and Tower Hill Roads and built a railroad spur extending down the southeast edge of Rattlesnake Swamp on the north side of what was eventually to be the Fox Hill Lakes. Crystal Lake was built first in 1893, with a 100-foot-long icehouse next to the

This small shed where the icehouse once stood is the last remnant of the Bell Labs sonar testing station that operated in the 1940s.

Our Lakes and Beaches

railroad tracks where the home on 28 West Shore Drive now stands. Sunset Lake was created several years later, its icehouse located along North Pocono Road. Birchwood was the third lake developed in 1905.[2]

Crystal Lake was developed in a swampy valley that had a large spring. The overflow filled Sunset Lake. Birchwood Lake relied on the runoff from the surrounding hills supplemented by a steam-driven pump on a flat car that drew water uphill from Crystal Lake to fill it. Eventually modern technology replaced the need for ice boxes and the Fox Hill Ice Company abandoned its ice harvesting business. By 1912 Hapgood had acquired the property with plans to build roads and housing around the lakes. It is believed Hapgood named the lakes; however, residents referred to them as Fox Hill Lake 1, 2, 3 (later called Upper Lakes 1, 2, 3). George Wilson remembers the lakes being called Howell's Ponds. One thing most agree on is that the ponds were numbered based on proximity; 1 being the closest (Sunset), 2 being Crystal, and 3 being the farthest away (Birchwood). There were other lakes as well, the names of which cause confusion and hearty debate. The Cove and the Reservoir are the most puzzling. Growing Up Laker, many of us referred to the far west end of Mountain Lake as the Cove. On maps however, the small pond between Overlook Road and Crane Road—what most of us call Propagation Pond—is the Cove. Across the Boulevard from the Cove/Propagation Pond is the Reservoir (according to the maps anyway). Do you recall anyone referring to it as that? It was always Grunden's Pond, then the Shaws claimed it as their own—Shaw's Pond. Well, no matter the names, we knew what lake we were talking about. Before the lakes, however, Mountain Lakes was just one big swamp! Ruth Doremus Watts, one of the original residents, moved with her family to Mountain Lakes in December 1911. *"We had lived on a farm in the summer months and my mother was an explorer. So, we used to drive up to Mountain Lakes and there were no lakes then. It was simply a great big swamp."*[1]

History pertaining to the smaller bodies of water—Shadow Lake, Olive Lake, Grunden's Pond, Propagation Pond (I'm sticking to the names I know) as well as the three lakes in the Lake Arrowhead neighborhood (Arrowhead Lake, Cooper Lake and Great Bay Pond)—is not readily known. Mountain Lake (the Big Lake) and Wildwood Lake were part of the original residential development plan. Once they cleared the beautiful chestnut trees to use for paneling in many of the houses in town, the areas were dug out further to create lovely recreational lake venues. Most of the early recreational activities took place on these two lakes—swimming, fishing, boating in summer; skating, ice sailing, curling, and hockey in winter. There were no designated spots to swim, so kids just made the best of it.

The Building of Our Beaches

There were no official public beaches in the early days of Mountain Lakes. Kids just swam at the closest lake. Myrtle Hillman Kingsley (b. 1915) learned to swim in Crystal Lake. *"There was a big rock about three feet out, so you could sort of jump from the shore to the rock and then go into the water and avoid those horrible leaves."*[1] For a while, there was a small beach on Sunset Lake on the corner of Pocono and East Shore Road. David Higgins notes that *"not too many people used it. My mother used to take us up there, until it was closed off for some underwater government work."*[1] (Bell Laboratories tested various sonar devices in Sunset and Crystal Lakes between 1941 and 1946). There was water access along the shore at the Mountain Lakes Club, but was it really considered a beach? *"The club had a small beach which was really not too good because of the location at the end of the lake and near the canal which was not used for swimming"* (Carolyn Carson Mills, '43).[1] Lack of an official beach changed when Mr. Leonard came on the scene.

Leonard's Beach

In 1924, E.J. Leonard opened a private beach on Wildwood Lake near the dam. He turned slippery grass banks and a mucky lake bottom into a broad white sandy beach complete with docks, diving boards, roped off swim areas, lifeguards, bathhouses, a retaining wall with wood slat benches, and a parking lot. He charged $10/year for family membership and issued metal badges, a tradition that continues to this day to indicate "belonging to the beach." According to some accounts, Mr. Leonard offered to sell the beach to the borough, but they weren't interested, possibly because of the high price.

Island Beach

The Borough of Mountain Lakes purchased Island Beach in the early 1930s and developed it as the first public beach (there's a 1933 beach tag in the ML Library's collection). According to David Higgins, *"it was a wooded area, a promontory that stuck out the way it does now. It was owned by a family named Kelly. We called it Kelly's Point."*[1] For the past 70-plus years, the beach has served us Laker kids well. We toddled around under the close (?) watch of our mothers, took swim lessons in the cold early mornings, passed our swim tests, launched sailboats from its shores, and got our first sunburns of the season. We headed down the steep drive by bike or foot, traversed the sharp, graveled parking lot and headed toward the beach. Under a canopy of large trees, we walked on cool sand—swings to the east, guard shack, restrooms, boat racks, and picnic tables to the west. The snack shack up ahead on the right—white stucco walls, dark green wooden "windows." We reach the bridge, stop at the large white wooden guard desk to show our badge, then cross over to the beach. A large oversized sand pile. One bench and two small trees at the far west end, parking for sailboats at the far east, monkey bars, two lifeguard stands, a flagpole, and that's it. Fish and pollywogs, young anglers with pole and red and white bobbers on one side of the island, swimmers and sunbathers on the other. In the water an old wood dock to the right and a modern aluminum dock to the left…all enclosed within the ropes that marked swimming territory. We could sail, canoe, or row our way to Island Beach from points beyond: Wildwood Lake via the Canal, the Cove, the Club, or the Midvale Boat Dock. Some of us even swam from the Boat Dock and the Club to Island Beach. It was the best summer place ever! But eventually, Island Beach had some competition.

Birchwood Beach

In the earliest decades of Mountain Lakes, Upper Lake 3 or Birchwood Lake as it would be called later, was just an ice pond surrounded by woods and railroad spur. Once abandoned by the Fox Hills Ice Company, Hapgood envisioned it as fertile ground for expanding Mountain Lakes Residential Community. Bankruptcy nipped that vision in the bud and Birchwood became a remote destination for kids seeking fun and an alternative swimming hole. From the 1920s through the 1950s kids trekked up there to swing from trees and drop into the deep waters. *"Sometimes the more adventurous would go to Birchwood and swim and have fun hanging onto a rope from a tree and swinging out over the water.*

There was no beach or dock there – just woods" (Carolyn Carlson Mills, '43).¹ George Wilson ('45) echoes the thought:

> *Birchwood was not a swimming lake, although we'd go up there to the third lake and swim. But the beach was across from where it is now. And then, where the concession stands are, about two big trees up, we had a rope, and you'd swing out over the water and drop. There's no way you could touch. I never saw water so deep. No one ever touched bottom, but they filled it in a lot when they put the docks in there. The man who put the docks in…Joe Klockner.¹*

Our Lakes and Beaches

The town was growing and thanks to Bill Kogen, Peter Haas, Sr. and others so were the summer recreation and swim programs. The town needed another beach to accommodate the burgeoning summer swim programs. A group of movers and shakers convinced borough officials to develop Birchwood as a community beach. So now we have a sandy beach carved out of the woods and a gravel path around the lake. To the east along the path are boat racks and picnic areas; to the west, the entrance to the beach guarded by the hallmark big white wooden lifeguard desk. Guard shack, showers and snack shack lined the entrance. Docks and swim lanes for swimming sent a message that competitive swimming was summer king—we would dominate Hub Lakes swimming for years and give the Lakeland Swim Conference teams a run for their money as well. Beyond this practice area was the beach with concrete retaining wall/seating area and wood docks, lifeguard stands, diving board, and water slide. Trees marked the west border and provided sanctuary from the afternoon sun. At the far end of the beach, beyond the monkey bars and swings, lily pads and leeches—the portal to prime fishing areas along its shores.

Birchwood was the beach for big kids—not as many families with crying little kids—except for Sunday afternoons when the handicap swim races were in full swing (handicap in the sense that the faster swimmers had a delayed start giving other swimmers a chance at winning the heat). Laker kids ruled the beach and the waters...well, until the lifeguards told us otherwise. It was a place of business—swim team workouts, diving practice, Monday and Wednesday night swim meets, Sunday handicap swim races. And, of course we can't forget home to Trout Derby! We could walk the path, get out of the sun, toss in a fishing line, launch a boat (not much boating action took place here though), sneak a smoke, and explore side trails that led to the Tourne and top-of-the-mountain neighborhoods. We camped overnight, caught fish, and cooked them over open fires...or we just ate the sandwiches and junk food we packed in from home.

Our Other Lakes

There were other lakes in town; some for swimming, some only fit for a boat and fishing rod. Crystal, Sunset, Olive, Shadow, Propagation, Grunden's, the Cove, and over in Lake Arrowhead neighborhood, Arrowhead Lake, Cooper Lake and Great Bay Pond were all part of our childhood playground. Every Laker kid who grew up on these lakes has a story, an adventure, a relationship with these waters. They were our private swimming and fishing arenas, or private skating rinks. We walked and waded along the shores, avoided swimming near the lily pads and jumped from wooden docks only. Except for Crystal Lake and a few spots on Shadow Lake (I can't speak for the rest of the lakes), rarely did we wade into the waters from the shore. We learned to bait a hook and cast our lines in these waters. With dogs as our companions, we honed our skills as sunny anglers. We hunted for turtles and frogs. We gathered the late summer green slime to toss at one another. We floated on rafts, canoes, and rowboats here. Four lakes (Crystal Lake, the Cove end of the Big Lake, Arrowhead Lake, and Great Bay Pond) boasted a special treat—small islands for kids to explore.

Bonnie Bedford Park captures life on the lake nicely. She lived on Crane Road in a house her father spent two years designing and building on the Cove to take full advantage of its majesty. She shares fond memories of life along the waters here:

Everyone who walked into our living room remarked on the "beautiful view" from the picture window looking out over "Birch Bay" (named for the birch trees circling the perimeter of the cove). As a kid, I would post watch from the window seat, where the wildlife seductively drew me into their world. Ducks, geese, swan and muskrats left their wake. Fish lurked below the surface – common pumpkinseeds and larger sunfish types, perch, bass, pickerel and catfish. Bull frogs hopped and splashed. Painted turtles bobbed. Giant snapping turtles occasionally culled a new brood of ducklings one at a time – we'd track the baby count under the watch of each mallard and if the number dropped the whole house heard about it – and the neighbors, too…I would frequently fish off the stone bridge on Cove Place. It was not uncommon to lose a hook or fishing lure on a lake bottom stump. One morning I ran inside to get my dad to help me unsnag my line. Always a sport, he climbed out of bed to assess the situation. "Stumps don't move," he said. We landed a giant snapping turtle, wrassled it into a canoe in the yard, and flipped it onto its back. Then called the police…Left unguarded, the monster I caught stuck out its very long neck, flipped itself over, crawled over the gunnel and escaped.[3]

Winter brought us other recreational delights on the lakes. When the white flag with the red ball was hoisted up the flagpole in winter, kids and parents alike poured out onto the lakes like ants to a picnic. Whether on the Big Lake or the smaller ponds, we graduated from double-bladed skates to figure or hockey skates. We left our boots and shoes behind and strengthened our ankles for the season. Dads cleared the ice for hockey rinks and kids got down to serious business. We played tag, crack the whip, and practiced our spins and jumps. We took shortcuts across the lakes rather than take the long way 'round in the bitter cold. But mostly we spent our time aimlessly skating, kind of like our walks around town. When our fingers and toes froze, we gathered around public and private fire pits to warm up or invaded friends' homes to thaw out, and then headed out to do it all over again.

Although some doubt it, many believe climate change does exist. In Mountain Lakes, anyway. When Mountain Lakes was in its early development, the Fox Hills Ice Company carved great blocks of ice from the Upper Lakes—Crystal, Sunset, and Birchwood—and sent them by rail to neighboring towns and businesses. And as a child of the 1960s and 1970s, I'm certain we skated and sledded from early December through March most years. Still, it seems these days there's not even enough time for a child to push a kitchen chair across the lake and master double-bladed skates.

My Favorite Lakeside Dwelling Places
(What's in your kaleidoscope of Growing Up Laker?)

Our Other Dwelling Places
Chapter Eight

Growing Up Laker, our hangouts changed based on season, age, and geographic location. Our circle of friends, interests, and parental permissions also influenced the haunts we frequented. What's unique is that despite social caste or athletic or academic inclination, boundaries were fairly fluid when it came to hanging out. In early decades, noted hangouts were schoolyards, the woods, locations along the lakes, and the Esplanade. Sports—organized and impromptu—were situated at Neafie's Field, then branched out to the Little League ball fields on Fanny Road, street hockey and basketball down behind the Market, and of course in any big neighborhood yard. As we got older, we cast our hangout nets even further to include the beaches, the bus stop, and the Wall. Schools and churches also opened their doors to kids through programs such as Canteen, Summer Recreation, and Chicago Molly's (the Coffee House).

Our Homes and Neighborhoods

"Every home has its own personality and spirit of place."
~Unknown~

Our homes were sprawling, three-story Hapgood four-squares, two-story Belhalls, and Cape Cods interspersed with split-level homes or one-story, mid-century modern anomalies. Didn't everyone have houses like ours? We slept there, ate there, played there, wore out our yards with neighborhood games, ventured hesitantly into damp basements to fetch laundry and canned goods or clean trout, and climbed up to cold or steamy third floors—depending on the season. These homes served as testing grounds for new ideas and talents, as way stations on our journey to and from school, and final destinations when the six o'clock siren went off or the streetlights came on.

Illustration of 105 Kenilworth Road (ca 1937) by Tom Stewart ('72).

While some homes were sanctuaries for parents and kids alike, others were full of rambunctious kids coming and going. They had revolving doors with welcome mats as big as the houses themselves. In the minds of parents with six, eight, ten children, what's another kid at the table? Those big breakfast nooks and formal dining rooms could easily seat ten or more. Other times the kitchens—with kitchen stools and breakfast tables—were places for after-school conversations with our moms, friends, and friends' moms. They were homework central long before computers, and holiday baking spots before the days of kitchen islands. And lest we forget, our kitchens were the primary location for one of two telephones in the house. Privacy while talking to our friends? Nope! Our kitchens, complete with breakfast nooks were indeed multipurpose informal hangouts.

Our big old houses had big old dining rooms and living rooms, often reserved for formal occasions. In our living rooms, our parents hosted formal cocktail parties and bridge parties. We practiced our piano lessons and listened to music on record players and hi-fi stereo systems. We had birthday parties in there—everyone spiffed up in their best party suits and dresses. Those living (and dining) rooms were big enough to host 6th grade sleepovers for at least a dozen girls! In winter we gathered around the fireplace—the only warm place in our drafty homes to hang out with family and friends.

Grander homes boasted of carriage houses, ballrooms, libraries, and sun porches for kids to explore. Complementing the expansive floorplans were wide sweeping stairways that climbed and turned to the second floor, then repeated the pattern on the way to the third. In the smaller Tudor homes, *"we had a huge and wonderful staircase to the second floor, with heavy oak carved and turned banisters and two landings along the way, perfect for spying down after bedtime upon my parents' parties* (Carolyn Farley, '64).[1] Many of these grand stairways had landings with back staircases leading down to the kitchen or up to the third floor. In earlier times only the live-in help travelled these back stairways, but for kids *Growing Up Laker*, they were alternate pathways for games of chase and hide-n-seek. Oh, and did your home have a dumbwaiter? Another memory worth stirring.

Our Hapgood homes had third floors which took on many functions throughout their lives. In early advertising floorplans, Hapgood's third floors were designed with rooms for live-in help and a billiard room. As rental and temporary spaces, they housed many different folks. During the Great Depression, kids shared their homes with strangers, teachers, and even neighbors who rented the top floor. Realtors often opened their homes to families waiting to move into their own newly purchased home (Peter Haas, Sr., '45; Tom Brackin, '53)[1] As economic times improved and families grew, kids claimed the third floor for playing, sleeping, and other mischief. We routinely practiced fire drills by tying sheets together, attaching them to the closet door handle, and climbing out to land on the porte-cochere roof. The final tricky part was climbing down the cedar trees that flanked the porte-cochere. Ouch! Finally, other families, like my grandparents just left the third floors unfinished as attic space making them perfect hiding places or teen hangouts (not like my grandparents!).

In the days before central heat and air conditioning, those of us who slept on the third floor suffered with the changing seasons—sweltering in the summer heat and humidity and freezing in the winter. In summer, we opened our windows, slept in next to nothing, prayed for the slightest breeze (the fans were of little use), and were lulled to sleep by the sounds of nature coming through the screens—katydids, frogs, crickets, and critters of all sorts. *"My bedroom was in the back of the house…I had a room of my own up in the attic…I loved to go to sleep with the peepers…Young frogs. And there were a million of them down there in those days. They sing you a song like you've never heard"* (Frank Wiswall).[1] In winter—well, you remember the routine: gather your brothers, sisters, dogs, sleeping bags and extra layers of pajamas to stay warm at night! It was the only time of year kids looked forward to warm baths and showers.

I have to take a detour here to talk about the furnaces in our old homes. These homes were originally equipped with coal-burning furnaces. I suppose the coal came from Dixon Coal yard right on the edge of town, but I can't be sure. The coal trucks backed up to the houses and dumped the coal down the chutes. Families needed to be sure to add just enough coal to keep houses warm at night. More importantly though was the need to keep windows open a bit to prevent toxic coal gas from building up in the house. Later, when coal furnaces were replaced with oil furnaces, the perils persisted. Both Abbie McMillen and Denis Waldron ('66) recall their oil furnaces exploding, spewing ash throughout the entire house. We had our own excitement at 333 Boulevard in the early 1970s. The furnace was on the fritz and Dad gave Mom a warning: "If the furnace starts making strange sounds, grab the kids and get out of there." Sure enough, while feeding the neighborhood kids lunch, the furnace started to rumble. It was no easy task getting several little ones and a non-English-speaking maid out of the house. Our neighbor Cliffie certainly wasn't in any hurry either; he was intent on finishing his lunch! Well, they all got out safely and there wasn't a single spot in that three-story home that wasn't covered in a coat of oily soot. Imagine coming out of class in high school and hearing a junior fire department member say, "Hey, your house just blew up!" I'm certain there are other exploding furnace stories out there.

Our big houses afforded us vantage points from where we could view the world…or our little piece of it. Sandy Faye Robinson ('58) recalls *"my window overlooked the driveway which was nice because I could keep track of my friends coming and going."*[1] When Carrie Shaw ('75) moved to a bedroom on the third floor, she could study at the built-in desk *"while looking into the tops of the trees at the birds in their nests."*[1] From my third floor room I could watch sailboats on the Big Lake, the sunset beyond Overlook Road, and the neighbors coming and going. I could sit on the window seat or at my desk and ponder life's mysteries…or what to wear to school the next day. Lorraine Lotti Wagner ('76) reflects *"as a young poet, I never ran out of inspiration in Mountain Lakes, and spent many a night perched in my third-story bedroom, looking out upon the intersection of Briarcliff Road and Glen Road, where I would write deep into the night."*[3]

We had wide, open porches and balconies on several sides of the house; safe places to play, read, make music, raise ducks, escape the sun. Carolyn Farley ('64) describes summertime on her porch.

Our living room ended with French doors that opened into a large screened in porch room facing out towards the point of our pie shaped property. In the summers, we would play endless games of poker out there in the porch-room until late at night, with not quite enough light to play by and crickets and katydids making their mysterious, but also comforting night noises, broken only by our laughter, while moths kept flying against the screens and lightning bugs twinkled outside.[1]

We also ate our summer meals on big screened in porches—bug free, shaded, with a wisp of a breeze now and then. Ah, but then the trend to turn every front porch into a TV room took hold. Goodbye screened-in porch, hello family room! Finally, balconies formed the roofs of our big porches and the function of these was simple—display

GAA signs every spring! (Okay, I confess. I did lug my telescope out there a few times to do some stargazing.)

As kids, we didn't spend much time indoors unless it was raining, or we were in trouble. We filled our days romping around in the yard, in the neighbor's yard or somewhere else in our easily traveled paradise. Our yards were big, some bigger than others. And in a town without fences kids combined their yards to create ball fields where there wasn't one big yard nearby. Each neighborhood had its own pod of kids and unique way of entertaining itself. You had clusters of kids from the Kenilworth-Melrose-Hanover area, Oak Lane-Barton Road-Briarcliff neighborhood, Larchdell-Dartmouth area, Diaper and York Villages, Lake Arrowhead neighborhoods, Crestview-Lookout-Condit Road area, and the Morris Avenue-Pollard Road-Lake Drive neighborhoods. I'm sure I missed a few. Tim Tensen ('74) remarks

> *Although ML is relatively small, each area of town had their own 'gangs' during that time due to our age and location... Guess you would consider ours the lower Laurel Hill/Tower Hill and little bit of the Boulevard gang. Sheas, Elmquists, McWilliams, Burnetts, Mills, Riordans, Merritts, Hamers, Sieberts, Reades, Barnes, etc. Probably 30-40 kids within a three-year age group.*[3]

Each neighborhood had its advantages too. Kids living close to schools got to sleep in and never experienced the first-period thaw that came after a two-mile walk to school on a frigid morning. Living up on the hill with sloping yards made for challenging play during temperate seasons but boasted some of the best sledding trails in town. But the ultimate place to live for any kid *Growing Up Laker* had to have been on the lake. Swimming, fishing, boating, and skating right outside your door! Whether you lived on the lake, up on the hill, or along well travelled roads, our homes were built for entertaining. And kids *Growing Up Laker* knew how to have a party.

Almost every kid *Growing Up Laker* heard about or attended the renowned weekend parties...grand affairs that lasted all night with loads of liquor charged to parents' accounts from the Market or

Worman's Liquor Store, cars parked everywhere along the streets and yards, loud music, and 100 or more close friends. Some were yearly events--New Year's Eve, Super Bowl, big sports wins, Saturday night after the GAA Show—or more likely just a celebration when parents went out for the evening or the weekend. Partygoers often helped clean up and destroy the evidence; however, if by chance, time got away from them or parents returned early, the guests would scatter, leaving their friend behind to explain things. Parties along the lake yielded other nerve-wracking results like losing clothes while skinny dipping and forgetting to put the car in park and having it roll into the lake. In those big houses with big porches and big yards, the parties never seemed too crowded. Certain homes around town were known for their parties. Take Club 95, for example. Scott Reynolds shares his story:

> *We lived at 95 Laurel Hill Road, and our house was the location of many underaged parties for many years, starting with me (MLHS 1959) and going through Gus (MLHS 1975). Our house became known as the Club 95. To this day, we still have cocktail napkins so inscribed. I understand our traditions were continued by the Keneally kids after my mother sold the house to them. The best parties happened when our parents were away, but there was usually incriminating evidence [and] swift justice when they returned.[3]*

Of course, there were quieter affairs—parties welcomed and hosted by parents. Teens swarming a friends' home and parents opening the refrigerators and cabinets to feed the hungry masses. Parents hosting pre-prom dinner parties and after-prom breakfasts for kids and their dates. Beyond these welcoming homes, there were many other *Growing Up Laker* hangouts. Let's explore!

Neafie's Field

Prior to the end of WWII, the Village, aka Diaper Village was a large meadow that kids turned into a ball field and adults later refashioned for school sports. In the earliest days, Ralph Osgood Wells and Robert

MacEwen recall the school (8th grade) had a baseball team and Mr. Milkey doubled as the baseball coach and music teacher. Jack Lee recalls his baseball days playing other teams in town. *"We had one called the Melrose Road Gang and they would play the Boulevards...We also played touch football on Neafie's field.*[1] When Briarcliff was built as the new high school, Neafie's Field served as the high school sports field for both football and baseball for a short while.

During summer, Neafie's Field was the place to be. As George Wilson ('45) notes,

when you got up in the morning, it was hot in the house, so you got the heck out of there... plus if you went home, your Mom wanted you to do yard work, or do this and that. And so, we'd walk down here under the bridge, and down the steps here. A little patch of woods, and then right field foul pole was right down here where these houses are.[1]

Neafie's Field offered a short cut and playground for those like Tom Brackin ('53) who lived on Intervale Road. His memories include the fire department's role in managing the field.

Kids loved it because the grass grew about as high as your nose and you could run through all these paths....The fire department felt it was a good idea to control the burn on the field...So they would come down and do a controlled burn in the fall, and all the firemen would turn out. They had trucks there...they let us light the fires. We had a grand time of it.[1]

Once World War II was over, the demand for affordable housing took priority over kids having fun. Mr. Fox turned Neafie's Field into what was dubbed Diaper Village. According to Buz Bedford, there were about 90 Cape Cod style houses built for veterans for about $9,900. Most were 1-1/2 stories with *"two bedrooms and a bath on the main floor and a dining room and kitchen."*[1] Buz goes on to explain how Diaper Village got its name: *"All the women were out hanging diapers because there were no electric dryers in those days. If you can imagine 90 lines with diapers on them. Every house had kids. We had 25 kids under five in one block. It exploded down there."*[1] The Village would expand to over 241

Our Other Dwelling Places

homes by 1953. While the Village homes were bursting at the seams with kids, just up the hill on the other side of the tracks and train station was a quiet little resting spot—the Esplanade.

Esplanade

Esplanade: "a long open level area typically beside the sea, along which people may walk for pleasure." No ocean in sight, just a railroad line and station. Early photographs of the Esplanade suggest it may have been developed as a welcome site for visitors arriving by train. It evolved into a park for wives and children awaiting husbands and fathers' return from work on the evening train. Over the decades, the Esplanade survived many cycles of splendor and disrepair, family-friendly vs teen trouble spots. As a hangout it was a place where teens do what teens do. It also served as a shortcut from the library to the Market. One of the noted events was the Peace Rally/Hippie Convention of 1970.

Saturday, 29 August 1970, the Esplanade was the venue for a peace rally (dubbed "Hippie Convention" by *The Citizen* newspaper). The announcement of this event sent a ripple of anxiousness through the hearts and minds of adults, police and town officials; a rash of vandalism and fire bombings in early August shattered the peace of our beloved town. Town officials weren't sure what to make of this upcoming convention.

A brand new police cruiser, Briarcliff School and Wildwood School were the targets of firebombs believed to be "reprisal against the establishment"—retaliation for a drug sting. The display windows of the Mountain Lakes Pharmacy were smashed as well. Since the makings of firebombs were found at the Esplanade—"200 bottles, two cans of gasoline, and an accumulation of rags...one of the bottles contained gasoline," no one was sure what to expect of the Hippie Convention. Organizers of the Peace Rally proclaimed

> *UNITE...We must struggle together and then raise our collective consciousness to where we can relate to our Brothers and Sisters fighting all over the Mother Country and to the international struggle for liberating all organizations, people, etc. wishing to form a coalition (for self-defense).*

In the end, the Peace Rally/Hippie Convention was indeed a peaceful affair. According to *The Citizen* article (4 September 1970), about 150 youngsters showed up to listen to rock music by Dan Rosler and Phil Peabody (the Orange Tarantula band), and to hear speeches by high school students, town residents, and a Vietnam veteran. Alumni Bill Riley and Jay Nelson arrived with a large barrel of fruit juice and a sign "Revolutionade 5-cents." When the gathering was over, teens returned to other familiar hangouts.

The Bus Stop and The Wall

The Bus Stop at the Northeast Corner of Lake Drive and Boulevard (near Martin's Lane) and The Wall were long-time roaming and resting spots in the 1960s and beyond, although the Wall seemed to outlive the Bus Stop as a popular hangout. And like the Esplanade, it was a place for teens to do what teens do. Robert W. Dunnican ('64) recalls *"hanging out at the bus stop (Lake Drive) talking about all the things we could do...and not actually doing anything."*

By day, the Wall was a waiting spot for the Good Humor ice cream truck. Kids crowded the sidewalk, dug in their pockets for saved allowances to buy ice cream—Fudgsicle, Creamsicle, Twin Pops, Chocolate Éclair, Toasted Almond, Drum Sticks and Ice Cream Sandwiches—we clamored to get our favorite. There are even tales of distracting our beloved Good Humor man Freddie to steal from the back freezer (damn kids!). But by night, especially on weekends and summertime, it transformed into a checkpoint of sorts, uniting teens from east and west, uphill and downhill. Tim Tensen remembers it as a time long before cellphones and such:

> *a time in a little town where people got together and kind of knew where people were going to be. Some were part time, others like me were there a lot. Of course, no cell phones or other ways to communicate once out of the house, so it was a place to either plan to meet or end up there because of others.*

Tim figures it *"was probably 10th grade and having the Seniors mainly hanging—Matt W., Sammy D., my brother, and many others. Most times we weren't allowed to sit, but that was the Seniors' game with us."* Yep, teens doing teen stuff—hanging out, talking a lot about nothing...or not talking at all. Passing the Wall and its denizens on my way to and from friends' houses, I hoped to be invisible so as not to evoke a "hello" to which I would have to stammer out a one-word reply. Returning decades later, I walked by and wondered, why didn't anyone ever sit on the wall across the street?

Other hangouts were more like destination locations—the Market, the Sweet Shop, Del's Village and its stores, and the library. We cruised through the Market at lunchtime for a sandwich from the delicatessen or candy and drink after school. We charged it to our parents' account if we didn't have any cash in our pockets. At times we would swing around down below to the Sweet Shop to visit with friends working there. A coke and an order of fries was all our unemployed financial status could afford. In the booklet, *Picturesque Mountain Lakes*, the area around the Market was billed as the business district of Mountain Lakes. *"Being centrally located in the town, it is within the reach of all residents. This assemblage of stores has a market, sweet shop, garage, tailor shop, hair dressers* [sic]*, post office, and clothing exchange"* (Correll and Koster 1958, 41).

Down at the other end of town was Del's Village, best known for back-to-school preparations and Sunday morning purchases of newspaper and donuts. *"Del's Village, two blocks from Mountain Lakes, is a modern shopping center used extensively by the residents. The popularity of this center is due to the wide variety of stores and excellent parking area"* (Correll and Koster 1958, 42). We visited some of those other shops too—Williams Stationery Store for candy and school supplies, the 5 & 10 Store for candy, cheap toys and miscellaneous stuff for school projects. There were many bike rides to the bakery for chocolate eclairs and visits with friends at the Brass Key…again, indulging in a teen feast of coke and fries if our pockets held the correct change. And when student projects or a thirst for reading struck us, we were off to the library. Ellen Gibson McGinnis ('78) sums up our fondness for the library this way:

The library! I could not wait to get my library card, and I used to take out as many books as they would let me (five at a time?), and bring them back two or three days later to get more. I remember story time when I was really small, and always stopping to see the miniature rooms in the front when I walked in. I can still smell the smell of that library.[3]

One final and important dwelling place (for the guys anyway) was the Mountain Lakes Fire Department.

Mountain Lakes Junior Fire Department

In the formative years of Mountain Lakes, the nearest fire station was in Hanover, an hour's drive away in those days (Skip Watts, '44).[1] It took five years before the town had a volunteer fire fighting force in operation. Over the decades they fought their share of fires, saved many homes, and experienced the loss of young lives. On 21 May 2016, the Mountain Lakes Volunteer Fire Department celebrated their 100th anniversary at the firehouse and included equipment displays and rescue demonstrations by members of the senior and junior departments. The shared stories about trainings, skillful drowning of fires, and fraternal gatherings in the clubhouse meeting room have contributed to this century of commitment. Critical to the success of the fire department in the early days was the establishment of the Junior Fire Department. Consisting of high school students, ages 16-18, it is still a large, active, and vital component to ensure the safety of the town and its residents. (Amy Stewart-Wilmarth, '74)

The Mountain Lakes Junior Fire Department was created during World War II, disbanded, and then re-established in 1969. Tom Stewart ('43) tell us

World War II started in earnest on December 7, 1941—Pearl Harbor was bombed by the Japanese. It became of great concern to all of us in high school since we knew we would probably become a part of it. Some of us joined the junior fire department in town and had training in firefighting. Mountain Lakes fire department was made up mainly of volunteers and of course some of the older members were going off to war.

Skip Watts devoted 50 years to the fire department, starting with membership in the junior fire department and has a similar memory.

Well, I started in 1941-correction-1942 as a junior fireman in high school, because in those days there were very, very few men in Mountain Lakes who were even here evenings because so many of the young men were away in the service. So the fire department decided that they would enlist a group of guys who were in high school and make us junior firemen with limited, you know-limited abilities to do things, limited authority to do things. And interestingly, to this day they have an extremely active junior fire department.[1]

The junior members fought right alongside the adult volunteers. Skip Watts recalls one of his experiences. "*Well, of course when I was a junior fireman, the market caught fire. And that was the first fire I have ever been involved in where there was a fatality. And that was odd. That was a long fire and it was just the kids....it was so cold. Oh God, it was cold.*"[1]

Fast forward 30 years and teenage boys were still serving. Deane Goltermann ('75) shares his memories of being a junior fireman.

These were guys who were generally not involved in sports, but you still had to be able to keep your hands and feet working together. We also had to be more or less available during the days, since that was our reason for being—to fill in with 'able' bodies when the big boys were stuck at work. Yeah, we got called out of school a couple of times.

Not only did the guys fill in when adult fire fighters were unavailable, their responsibilities also extended to the care and operation of equipment. According to Deane, the auxiliary truck was the prime training rig—"*a 1946 model with tricky gearshift and incredibly weak engine. I still recall the first lesson—'You're in control, don't be afraid. Hold the stick like it's your girlfriend's breast—firm but gentle.' We also got to learn how to start the truck uphill…('you never know where the fire will be'). We'd drive to the steepest roads…park with emergency brake and turn the engine off. The exercise was to get that old truck going from a standstill. We learned to drive a stick, in any case.*"[3]

Membership in the Mountain Lakes Fire Department crossed family and generational lines. Fathers, sons, brothers, and cousins worked side by side to keep our town and highly combustible homes from burning to the ground. Along the way these young men learned life lessons about brotherhood and community service. Other ways Laker kids learned about camaraderie and cooperation was through self-generated clubs.

Our Clubs and Alliances

As kids *Growing Up Laker*, we had endless ways to entertain ourselves and others. We formed clubs to explore common interests, play sports, and channel our creativity. Neighborhood clubs sprung up, each as curious and varied as the next. Bonnie Bedford ('74) notes "*With the neighbor kids, I rode bikes up and down Cove Place. Together we formed a 'Bicycle Safety Club.' Bulbous horns adorned our handlebars.* [We] *also* formed a 'Squirrel Club,' the initiation—eating part of an acorn—bitter but not toxic."

The most common self-led organizations were social clubs, sports leagues, and teen bands. Although schools offered a club for every imaginable interest, we could only participate during school-designated hours. We were a restless bunch *Growing Up Laker*; a social bunch. When school was out, we created our own pastime pleasures. For example, Amy's father, Thomas Stewart ('43) formed the Penguin Club with his friends.

Fraternities were among the many high school sponsored clubs. By day, they were civic minded organizations. However, by night, these fraternities were social clubs that hosted their fair share of parties around town. The Penguin Club, however, was one of a few stand-alone social clubs that formed outside high school boundaries. Amy shares her father's notes about the Penguin Club in his memoirs. Her father moved to Mountain Lakes in time for his freshman year of high school. In his memoirs, he writes,

> *By my junior year there were six of us that were doing a lot together. When the high school was built in 1936 my friend Wes's folks bought one of the construction sheds and had it moved to their back yard. They had a patio built in front of it, pine paneled the shed and had a fireplace with a hearth-built in. The shed was probably 10 feet by 15 feet and this is where we had many parties. It got to be known as the Penguin Club which was derived from a lot of small animal figurines on the mantel piece.*

According to Amy, members of the Penguin Club *"remained close friends through the years until their deaths. Always picking up where they left off at annual get-togethers and high school reunions. A familiar feeling to many of us."*

Thomas Stewart ('43) and fellow Penguins their senior year.

We formed friendships through our membership in these various clubs. Neighborhood sports were no different. Take the Mountain Lakes Street Hockey League and the game of Stuff Basket for instance. According to Steve Delchamps ('74), street hockey came to town in the winter of 1972. The game is like ice hockey with a few differences—shoes instead of skates, ball in lieu of puck. It took some experimentation to get the tools of the game right. His article in the March

1973 issue of *The Mountaineer*, the high school newspaper, provides the details:

> *Local involvement in the sport began around the winter of '72 when several areas around town fashioned crude teams of inept, inexperienced players who gladly participated. Development was slow. At first, goals were two rocks. Sticks were wooden and broke easily. The forwards couldn't pass or shoot, and there was frequent tripping, bruising and swearing. Goalies were reluctant kids who figured that someone had to do the nasty job of standing in front of bouncing, rock-hard tennis ball and the dirt, cinders, and rocks that invariably followed, and trying to stop the damned thing.*

As the game evolved, they replaced make-shift equipment with real street hockey implements and built real goals. Richard Lotti ('74) notes *"I think the boards came from Culberston's house and the goalie nets were made of steel piping from my Dad's company. Apparently, those nets were handed down over the next twenty years and often showed up in wintertime on Mountain or Wildwood Lake."*[3] The players also tested out various playing surfaces in town including Roberts' field on 100 Ball Road, the basketball courts by Schultz's Garage, and according to Steve *"macadam enjoyed brief popularity, but veteran players longed for the dirt field, with its boulders sticking up all over the place, and the clouds of choking dust, all of which had become their life media"* (Delchamps, March 1973). Eventually the boys would discover the joys of playing on tennis courts and indoor gyms.

By spring and summer of 1972, the Mountain Lakes Street Hockey League had four teams: The Saucers from Ball Road, the neighboring Flyers, the Crystal Road area team, and Pollard Road team. Team leaders and players included Dave Delchamps, Steve Manson, Steve Delchamps, Rich Lotti, and John Walters Doug Ceva, Doug Riker and Bob Leland, Kim Mueser, Dag Hellandjo, Tom Soldat, Jim Murphy and Jim Crotty. These players were joined by college hockey veterans Jim

Carrier and Dave Maddox who brought a new level of grit and expertise to the game. Steve notes that it was Jim Carrier's ties to school officials that enabled the league to move indoors and play in the Lake Drive School Gym.

The Mountain Lakes Street Hockey League was born from a common passion for the sport and fueled mostly by players who were not members of organized school sports. The result—year round fun, honest rivalry and sportsmanship, and enduring friendships that were formed in the name of good and maybe not so clean fun on those street hockey fields.

Let's Go Play Stuff!

Another popular game in the 1970s was Stuff Basket. Amy's brother Tom Stewart ('72) fills us in on the details.

We would look for ten guys, no real set teams and play 5 on 5, sometimes 4 on 4. The teams were primarily made up of guys from the classes of '71, '72 and '73. The stuff basket was made with a 4x4 post, backboard and rim which was ONLY nine feet high. Typically set up on a cul-de-sac. There were two stuff baskets, we played full court and we used a volleyball. We felt like professionals because we could palm the volleyball and dunk it! We did not let kids on the high school basketball team play; otherwise anyone could join in. There were a few courts scattered around that I remember; I usually played on the court near York Road with David Dean, Turner Prewitt, David Carrier, and others. We would say, "let's go play stuff!" It was a lot of fun.

Informal sports groups provided opportunities for kids of all skill levels and an outlet for good old-fashioned fun. Other groups with shared passions also took hold in Mountain Lakes, such as teen bands.

Teen Bands

Like most towns and cities, Mountain Lakes had teen bands. What's unique is the explosion of bands that took over our small town in the 1960s. There were a musicians and bands playing a few venues in town—dances, canteens, and such. Rick Sigman ('74) provides a glimpse into this emerging phenomenon in his essay "Memories of the Music Scene in Mt. Lakes – Early '60s to Early '70s." (The entire essay is in the Historical Essays collection on the Mountain Lakes website). According to Rick, Buzz Clifford, the Catalinas (Bill Carlin, Mark Babyak and Buddy Rizzio), and the Riffs (Frank Sugrue, John Elerath, Kells Elmquist and Dave Thomson) started things off.[2] But after that historic Sunday night—9 February 1964—when the Beatles debuted on the Ed Sullivan Show, a tsunami of teen bands comprised of creative and entrepreneurial music devotees flooded the town. Rick writes

> *Mt. Lakes in the 1960s saw a sudden explosion of kids wanting to learn to play the guitar, drums, and piano/keyboards. We started forming bands as a new era of music hit the airwaves. In February 1964, we were fixated on our black and white TVs as the Beatles exploded on the music scene with their first performance on the Ed Sullivan Show. It was arguably the single, most influential moment in time for a new era of music. I point to that moment when I, along with so many other kids, wanted to be just like the Beatles. The Beatles in the early '60s ushered in a new wave of clothing, hairstyles, attitudes, and of course, music.[2]*

The Scorpions (Sten Stovall, Paul DiCarlo, Artie Heissenbuttel, Jeff Hitt, John O'Conner) formed shortly thereafter serving as *"ground zero of the Mt. Lakes Rock 'n' Roll music scene."*[2] Many more kids followed suit and formed bands of their own. Rick continues the story:

> *As the number of bands in Mt. Lakes grew, we sought out places we could perform live. We started playing at the local canteens, dances, parties and churches. Lake Drive School, Briarcliff School, Mt. Lakes*

High School, Community Church, St. Peter's and St. Catherine Church became our stage to play Rock & Roll music. In 1966 I was recruited by Bobby Duff to start a band. We were called the Night Riders. Bobby Duff, Dale Richey, Cal Pickens and Eddie Hope and me. Our first gig was at the Community Church (I remember Bobby's mother bought us all matching red ties). To our dismay, there was another band there also. Billy Thatcher had formed his own band, Billy and the Kids. Billy, Jay Elder and Dave Coogan. They played first and sadly for us they were better. Much better...

We licked our wounds and in April of 1967 the Night Riders got 3rd place in a "Battle of the Bands" at the Bonanza Steak Pit in Bloomfield, NJ. The 3rd place prize was a whopping $5.00. Each of us earned a dollar. Many years later I found an old envelope my mother saved with the first dollar I made playing music.[2]

By all accounts there were around 19 bands that emerged in the 1960s and early 1970s: The Catalinas, The Riffs, The Scorpions, Meditation, The Motley Crew, Billy and the Kids, Frenetic Movement, The Deadbeats, The Night Riders, Northern Lights, Lang and Brian, No Name Band, Home Brew, Bill and Annie, Orange Tarantula, Forest, Desert Thunder, Hobo Gulch and Nebula. Music is still a core element in many of these musicians' lives to this day.

Our Churches

There were three main churches kids spent time at in Mountain Lakes: the Community Church on Briarcliff Road, St. Peter's Episcopal Church on the corner of Martin's Lane and the Boulevard, and St. Catherine of Siena Catholic Church on North Pocono Road. The Community Church of Mountain Lakes was the first to open its doors on 14 December 1914. Serving the spiritual needs of Mountain Lakes residents for over 100 years, it has been a second home for annual bazaars, scouting, ballroom dance, youth groups, and coffee houses.

Community Church (top).
St. Peter's Episcopal Church and St. Catherine of Siena Catholic Church (bottom).

For many years the Community Church hosted a UN Weekend. Kim Westfall Cayes ('75) recalls

> *My great Aunt Beulah and Uncle George hosted for that weekend and organized exchanges for years and years through the Experiment in International Living. It gave me great exposure to all kinds of cultures. But yes, that square dance for the United Nations weekend was the best!"*[4]

St. Peter's Episcopal Church was built eight years after the Borough of Mountain Lakes was founded due to the efforts of the Reverend Henry B. Wilson, rector of St. John's Episcopal Church in nearby Boonton. Over the many decades, not only has it played a vital role in the religious education and spiritual development of kids *Growing Up Laker*, it has been the venue for scouting, youth groups, and great seasonal bazaars and book fairs. Finally, St. Catherine of Siena Catholic Church came along in the mid-1950s. Catholic families were looking for a place to call their own. Temporary venues included the Mountain Lakes Club with over 425 attending the first mass in July 1956, and then renting larger space from the Masonic Temple at Island Beach for Sunday and Holy Day services. Finally, the town celebrated Christmas Eve mass in its new home in 1958. (Midnight Mass became the final stop of the teenage tradition of attending all Christmas Eve services in town). Every Catholic teen spent afternoons in catechism class at St. Catherine's (with the occasional skipping out to Paul's Diner). Mountain Lakes now had a third venue for kids *Growing Up Laker* to worship and learn and spend time with friends in organized activities.

Growing Up Laker, we spent time in church with our families—we were spectators and students at first. As we got older, we participated in services as acolytes, teacher aides in the nursery, singers and handbell ringers in the choirs. Our churches not only provided spiritual guidance, they also served Laker kids by hosting a variety of community activities. Here we focus on *Growing Up Laker* activities of scouting, youth groups, ballroom dancing, and coffee houses.

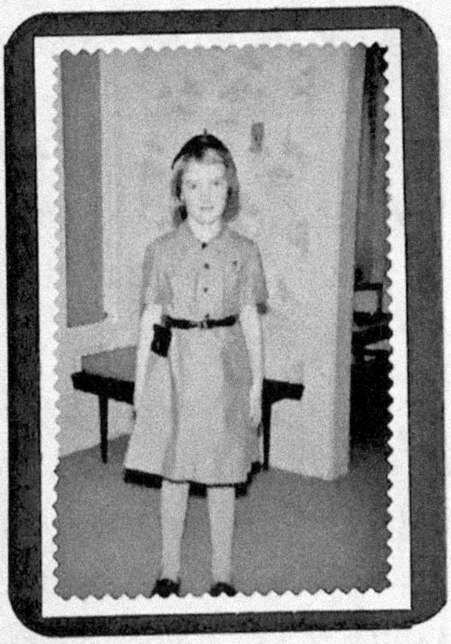

Scouting

Nothing says church life for a kid *Growing Up Laker* like Scouting. Every church hosted its share of Cub Scouts, Boy Scouts, Brownies, and Girl Scouts. Every week we met, got a little lecture, worked on projects and badge requirements, and planned big outings. It seemed to me that while the boys did a lot more <u>doing</u>, we did a lot more <u>sitting</u>, listening and watching. And while the boys seemed to venture out into the woodlands of Mountain Lakes to hone their survival, camping, and pioneer skills, we girls were sequestered like a jury within the church walls. I comb through the cobwebs of my scouting memories and fail to recall journeying into local woods; only trips to distant places (mostly in winter) where we remained under close watch of overprotective scout leaders. Wandering off on adventures with other renegade scouts resulted in a sound scolding and latrine duty as punishment. When we got a bit older, there were youth groups to keep us occupied.

Youth Groups

Church Youth Groups were a popular meeting place for kids. The goal was to give kids a safe place to hang out and have fun. David Higgins (b. 1922) remembers:

> *We used to have what they used to call Young People's [Society], at the Community Church. It was run by a young fellow—he was probably eight to ten years older than the children. We went once a week—I think it was Saturday. It was primarily dancing. I think he had soft drinks. There were records playing. Old 78 rpms. Big band music primarily.*[1]

In the late 1960s and early 1970s, the 78 rpm records were replaced with 45s (we wore those Sonny & Cher songs out!). I don't remember much else about the time I spent there on Sunday afternoons, but the Young People's program continued to provide a place to hang out regardless of religious affiliation.

Ballroom Dance

Carolyn Farley ('64) recalls the ballroom classes held at the Community Church on Saturday evenings in the late 1950s, early 1960s:

> *Girls were to be dressed in semi-formal and formal gowns and gloves, boys in suits and ties. We were taught to waltz, fox trot, cha and behave with gentility and civility toward each other. We sometimes had dance cards, wherein the number of dances of the evening were listed and the boys went around and signed up for a specific dance with the girls of their choice until all the dances were promised. Then, in turn, the boys would turn up to claim their dances. The resulting full cards hung by ribbons or strings from the girls' gloved wrists and were taken home as souvenirs…Can you imagine 12-to 14-year-olds of today at such an activity?*[1]

Abbie McMillen recalls dance lessons too: " *It must have been gruesome to watch, and it was awkward (to say the least) to participate in, but in the end, the memories are of sweet chivalry and good manners.*"[1]

By the late 1960s, gone were the formal dresses, dance cards and ribbons, but the requirement for girls to wear dresses and gloves and boys to wear suits and ties remained. A marvelous thing for girls happened in 8th grade—we graduated from white anklets to stockings! Girls still sat with ankles crossed, while boys retrieved the refreshments and asked for the next dance. Box Step, Fox Trot, Lindy, Cha-Cha, Waltz, all done to music on a record player. And once in a great while, as reward for dance step mastery, we got to break out and dance to a modern tune from the juke box stationed along the back wall. Another treat was travelling to Smoke Rise to dance with their class (who knew there was such a thing as gated communities). We danced on Saturday nights during the school year, and for some it was the longest hour of their short lives. Well, ballroom dance lessons wouldn't last forever—pretty soon sashaying around the dance floor was replaced with swaying to groovy sounds in the coffee house downstairs. We were growing up!

Chicago Molly's

Chicago Molly's, a coffee house in the basement of the Community Church opened its doors in 1969. Rick Sigman ('74) provides some history.

> *In 1968, the Ressler family moved into Mt. Lakes next to the Community Church. Mr. Ressler was director of the Lakeland Hills YMCA and director of youth programs at the Community Church. Knowing the church basement was unused, brother and sister, Bill and Annie Ressler (avid folk musicians) had an idea to turn the abandoned basement into a "Greenwich Village style" coffee house like they had seen in NYC. Annie and Bill pitched the idea to their father as a community service and the Community Church agreed to give them the keys.*

Bill and Annie, Mike O'Malley, and a handful of students and parents began the coffee house project. All the labor on the coffee house project was by volunteers and almost everything was donated. Large wooden cable spools for tables, any chairs they could find, candles in colorful glass holders and purple paint for the walls (the only color they could get for free). Bruce Yaw, another local musician, offered the coffee house his old P.A. system.[2]

It took many hands to manage Chicago Molly's. According to an article in *The Citizen* newspaper (17 September 1970), church youth group and committee members for the 1970-71 season included (in alphabetical order): Kevin Avery, Susan Baldwin, Dick Barnes, Dotty Bedford, Libbie Counselman, Carol Erikson, Sue Hale, Cam Klockner, Janet Leef, Laurie Campbell, Dave Goodacre, Cathy McCann, Bernie McGovern, Alison Roy, Ann Yoder, Nancy Zufall. There were many other volunteers over the years of Chicago Molly's operation.

So how did they arrive at the name? Rick Sigman explains the founders wanted a name that *"would get people's attention but had nothing to do with the church or the town. It was Betty Ressler, their mother who suggested "Chicago Molly's One Night Stand."*[2]

Chicago Molly's boasted a venue for live music—folk, blues, and jazz—and simple snacks. The coffee house was open twice a week during the summer and Friday nights during the school year. Chicago Molly's offered an inexpensive entertainment outlet for Laker teens for several years. With an admissions table at the entry way, a concession area in the corner (coffee, cocoa, bagels), small stage up front, and tables made from industrial-sized spools, we paid our admission and settled in to the smoky den to listen to some of the finest local, live music around.

Growing Up Laker afforded us many dwelling places—places to play, explore, relax, ponder life's mysteries, or just plain hang out. These were sacred spaces for kids...some of them shared by many; others a secret spot deep in the woods or along the shores to call our very own.

My Favorite Dwelling Places
(What's in your kaleidoscope of Growing Up Laker?)

Part III

Preserving Our Heritage and Homes

Madame Belle de Rivera, early resident, pioneer, suffragette, and colorful character was invited to address the attendees of the 25th Anniversary Ball on the 5th of June 1936.

> *Twenty-five years have come and gone and brought great changes, but the love for our lakes and mountain remain the same. A man had a vision. And we have lived to see that ideal become a reality, and with this realization has come the responsibility to carry on what was so well begun and brought to its present success. (Herold 2010, 102-103).*

Between the inception of Mountain Lakes Residential Park and Hapgood's departure, 482 homes had been built. But by the end of 1922, Hapgood was in financial difficulty, having overextended himself in the building of the borough, its houses, and its infrastructure. Some of the financial difficulty could be attributed to Hapgood's claim that Mountain Lakes residents owed $40,000 in past due accounts, a hefty sum in those days. Saddled with enormous debt, Hapgood skipped town for South America, leaving his family, the scandal of bilking his father-in-law out of $60,000, and the dream of Mountain Lakes Residential Park behind.

Hapgood's departure raised panic regarding the status and future of Mountain Lakes as a community. The Belhall Construction Company offered to buy and complete the unfinished homes. The Belhall Company built approximately 60 homes in a new style of architecture. Unlike Hapgood's sprawling Craftsman style homes, these were smaller homes in the English and Colonial Tudor style. But the Belhall Company landed on hard times during the Great Depression. According to the booklet, *This is Mountain Lakes*, the company *"fell into financial difficulties and paid no taxes on the great bulk of its land holdings from 1931 on"* (1954, 8). In 1937 the courts established a trust, liquidated the company's assets, and satisfied the lien placed on the holdings by the Borough of Mountain Lakes. By 1939, the borough was able to buy mortgages totaling $700,000 for only $1,700. Residential development was back on track, *"but [the transaction] served another important purpose: 'We controlled the future development of Mountain Lakes in a way which zoning laws and deed restrictions could never have controlled,' said [Mayor] Mr. Frederic, 'because we owned it'"* (*This is Mountain Lakes* 1954, 8).

Ownership and control over the town's destiny and development would continue to exert visionary influence throughout the borough's life.

In the mid-1940s, the town expanded and "Diaper Village" was built to provide affordable homes to returning veterans and their families. This neighborhood featured two-story Cape Cod style homes. Mountain Lakes continued its expansion; in the 1950s, modern mid-century style homes were springing up in between the Hapgoods and Belhalls.

These were our homes and our town *Growing Up Laker*—the Hapgoods, the Belhalls, the Cape Cods, and the mid-century moderns—this is where we lived and played. And we wanted it to remain the way our founders intended. In the 1967 booklet, *This is Mountain Lakes*, the authors reiterate this philosophy to its readers and future residents.

The prevailing policy since 1956 has been not to sell Borough-owned property for building sites. Through the years there has been a strong feeling here to maintain the original character of the town and, therefore, there has been marked resistance to new housing developments, apartments, or industry. (9)

Testing the Laker Spirit

Hapgood's vision of a residential park and the Spirit of Mountain Lakes were tested in the mid-1980s through the 1990s. The bigger-is-better trend followed by new homeowners and home builders was pushing the Mountain Lakes landscape away from its original intent of a residential, natural-surroundings environment to one of ostentatious displays of vanity. Thankfully there were town leaders who believed in the heritage and Spirit of Mountain Lakes and initiated steps to preserve the town and protect it from developmental blight. The historical significance of the Hapgoods and Belhalls—but mostly the Hapgoods—was such that Mountain Lakes officials launched a four-year campaign to secure a place on the State and National Registers of Historic Places to preserve the homes and the original vision of Mountain Lakes Residential Park.

The Borough's Response:
Preservation, Restoration, Duplication

According to the Mountain Lakes Historic Preservation Committee (HPC)

> *The nomination to become an historic district was prepared by the HPC at the request of the Borough Council. The preparation took from 2001 to 2005 and involved approximately five dozen volunteers from town. The community volunteers and HPC committee members spent countless hours documenting our town in words, photographs, maps and slides; and researching the town's history. The final document individually describes over 1,700 properties and is in excess of 300 pages. A copy of the full nomination can be found at the library and at Borough Hall.* (ML HPC, National and State Historic District, para. 2)

The fruits of their labors were realized and in 2005 the Mountain Lakes Historic District was listed on the State and National Register

of Historic Places. Former Mayor Stephen Shaw ('78) notes that the decision to pursue the Historic District designation was not without its concerned citizens. He explains that one concern was the effect historic designation rules would have on borough owned public buildings and lands. Obtaining Historic District designation meant obeying strict guidelines for not only house modifications and building decisions, but also for the development of community areas such as parks, beaches, etc. Stephen admits in hindsight that the historic designation was a good thing. The borough's website elaborates on the significance of its nomination and designation.

> *The National Register of Historic Places is the nations' official list of cultural resources worthy of preservation...part of a national program to coordinate and support public and private efforts to identify, evaluate, and protect our historic and archeological resources. To qualify for listing, properties must be significant in American history, architecture, archeology, engineering, or culture.* (ML HPC, National and State Historic District, para. 5)

> *Mountain Lakes qualifies as an historic district under the primary criteria of significance of community planning and development as a planned residential park suburb. The secondary criteria are significance in architecture, for the concentration of Craftsman style homes. The planned residential park suburb designed by the developer Herbert J. Hapgood with his landscape designer Arthur Holton has been maintained to the current time....Out of an original 482, there are 451 remaining Hapgood houses at this date, and 57 Belhall homes out of approximately 60 originally built.* (ML HPC, National and State Historic District, para. 7)

Mountain Lakes was conceived as a planned residential park with man-made lakes, sweeping backdrops of steep hills and defining puddingstone walls and pillars. The town's 102 years has taken its toll on these historic dwellings through economic and environmental changes and architectural trends. To publicize the historic district designation, the Historic Preservation Committee offers for purchase historic plaques for both the Hapgood and Belhall homes (Amy Stewart-Wilmarth, '74).

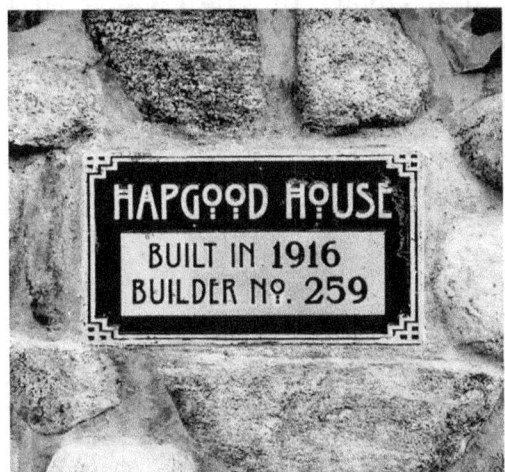

In the years since the historic district designation, the Borough of Mountain Lakes has devised policies to protect the integrity of the historic homes while giving homeowners as much freedom as the historic district rules permit. In 2012 the Mountain Lakes Borough Council approved a new ordinance to encourage owners of historic homes to consider preservation with broader zoning incentives when wanting to make changes on their home. In 2017 changes were adapted by the council to make it even more appealing for homeowners. The ordinance was proposed to the council by a few local builders due to an increased trend to demolish the historic Hapgood and Belhall homes. To further assist homeowners in the preservation of these historic homes, an architectural salvage program was started by the Historic Preservation Committee for the storing of architectural details removed from Hapgoods and Belhall homes during renovations or prior to unfortunate demolitions. These stored articles are available to Mountain Lakes homeowners to use for renovations on these historic homes. The storage building located in town was renovated in 2017 and is called the Preservation Shed (Amy Stewart-Wilmarth, '74).

Several Mountain Lakes builders and real estate developers such as Stephen Shaw ('78) and Tom Menard ('84) strove to preserve and restore the existing homes. When they were beyond salvaging, new ones were built in their place in the Hapgood style. Amy notes that Tom Menard, a longtime resident of Mountain Lakes and home builder has restored "over 100 original Hapgood's and has lived in at least ten." He has also built new Hapgoods in both Boonton on Fanny Road and in Mountain Lakes. The Fanny Road property became available and he named it "Hapgood Court" in honor of Hapgood and Mountain Lakes. Both the Boonton and Mountain Lakes homes mimic the original Hapgood designs. Some of the interior trim matches the original Mountain Lakes Hapgoods, however, the current costs for replicating the woodwork is not affordable for all homeowners. Many of the new Hapgoods built in Mountain Lakes replaced split level homes that were no longer popular.

The efforts of Mountain Lakes citizens and the Historic Preservation Committee extend far beyond protecting the historic buildings in Mountain Lakes. They are engaged in protecting our Laker heritage, our Laker Spirit. While Hapgood created the vision for our residential community, the founding citizens arrived with perseverance and ignited a Laker Spirit that transcends the decades and overcomes various challenges. Perhaps this same spirit and perseverance bolstered you in the midst of troubling times or when you sensed your mettle being tested. Did you call upon that Laker Spirit—the values, morals, and lessons we gained from *Growing Up Laker*— and rise to the occasion? I imagine you did.

Part IV

❁ ❁ ❁ ❁ ❁

Growing Up Laker
Final Thoughts

Thanks for joining us on this journey through 70 years of *Growing Up Laker*. Did you enjoy travelling through the school year experiencing the spirit of the season in our town? Did revisiting old haunts and dwelling places stir memories of your own times in these special spaces? Were you transported back, even for just a moment, to a time of innocence, wonder, and unadulterated fun? We hope so. There are as many stories as there were kids *Growing Up Laker* during those first 70 years and no composition can capture all the stories of its characters. We left some pages blank in this collective memoir for you to share your own tales. Please do. We also hope someone else picks up where we left off and compiles memories of the ensuing 40 years.

As you conjure up your kaleidoscope of Laker memories do you see, smell, and hear the changing spirit of the season? Do you see the colors emerge, then fade and transform? The bright spice colors of fall reflected on smooth waters; black, white and grays interspersed with sparkling silver; new, pale splashes of color against dark soil; dark greens of the woods, the twinkling of lightning bugs, colorful sails against a watery backdrop. Do you smell the autumn fires, the winter feasts and baked goods, the lilac bushes of spring, and the heavy fragrance of lake, lawn, and sweat of summer? Do you hear the crunch of leaves and acorns, the crack and boom of expanding lake ice, the silence of the holiday nights, the songs of returning birds and hatchlings, the

echoing of "Marco…Polo," the serenade of the peepers, katydids, and crickets? When the spirit of the season comes full circle, seek the spirit of your favorite dwelling places through these kaleidoscope memories.

Do you feel the energy of football games with the entire town in the stands; the wonder while alone with your skates and your lake on a starlight night? Are you searching for your favorite campsite or fortress deep within the woods, or staking a claim along the shores on a cool April morning in hopes of catching the coveted Golden Trout? Feel the thrill as you swing high and drop from the rope into the chilly waters of Crystal Lake; or catch that strong wind, hold the rope tight, lean back on the boat, and sail the length of the Big Lake. Perhaps you just want to hang out—simply hang out—at the Wall, the bus stop, the school yard, your favorite rock, the ballfields, a friend's house, or on your own big porch. Wherever you are, does the Laker Spirit call to you like some ancient chant and lure you back?

Growing Up Laker and the connection we have calls to mind a family tree. Whether by birth or relocation once we arrive in Mountain Lakes, we are family. We are rooted by a common denominator that is the indefinable Laker Spirit. Its branches support us through brilliant minds, artistic hands, and an ethos of work hard, play hard, respect and care for others, honor your heritage and natural surroundings. Some of us join the generations who remain to raise their own families here, some return after a long absence, and some discover towns around the world that are characteristic of Mountain Lakes. Some of us are still searching for that elusive place. Wherever we are, we are rooted in our collective experience *Growing Up Laker*.

We either loved it or hated it, but eventually we found peace with growing up in Mountain Lakes. And it was good. We recall our childhood days through aged and tempered minds, and the mosaic is precious. It's our youthful experiences in that indescribably unique community that made us who we are today. For that we should be thankful. Lorraine Lotti Wagner ('76) notes *"Each of us carries a jewel within us; sparkling like the sun on those lakes."*[3] This jewel we carry, this thing that's woven into our soul, is the Laker Spirit. And it's this Laker

Spirit that rises from kaleidoscope memories and leads our hearts to sing *"No matter where we wander or wherever we may roam, we will always think of Mountain Lakes as home!"*

The Alma Mater
Mountain Lakes High School

(Words by George H. Littell, Music by Ted Milkey)

When all Mountain Lakers gather
It is never very long
Till we praise our Alma Mater
With a song.
As we join our hearts together
Raise our voices clear and true
In allegiance to the orange
And the blue!
Sing! Sing! The Mountain Lakers' song
To thee, our loyal hearts belong
For no matter where we wander
Or wherever we may roam
We will always think of Mountain Lakes as home!
Where the echoes from the hillsides
Ring around the Wildwood Shore
Dwell a host of friends we'll cherish evermore
Though our paths may someday sever
We'll recall the happy throng
That was bound as one together in a song.
Sing! Sing! The Mountain Lakers' song
To thee, our loyal hearts belong
For no matter where we wander
Or wherever we may roam
We will always think of Mountain Lakes as home!

About the Authors

Susan Barnes is a life-long analyst and researcher with an insatiable curiosity. Susan grew up in Mountain Lakes, New Jersey—a unique community with an indefinable spirit and bond that just had to be explored. Unravelling this mystery from a kid's perspective became her first adventure as an author. She is an Air Force veteran of 25 years, an adjunct social work professor, a Haiku dabbler, and a costumer for an historic village and two community theaters in her area. She lives in Florida, yet longs for the mountains and woods of her youth.

About the Authors

Amy Stewart-Wilmarth has reveled in writing and photography as ongoing paths for expressing sentiments, life happenings and capturing nature's beauty since young adulthood. She exhibits at the annual Leonard J. Buck Garden Art Exhibit in NJ and her photography was published online in 2007 and 2012. She wrote and photographed her first book, Along the Morris Canal in 2014.

Amy supports her love for creativity and exploration with her degree in Nursing and BA in Psychology. She is also a certified Holistic Health Coach and has focused her nursing career on nutrition, prevention and senior advocacy. She presently works for an organization as their Health and Wellness Director.

Amy lives in Oak Ridge, New Jersey and enjoys the outdoors including being a longtime supporter of organizations dedicated to protecting marine life on the East Coast.

Notes

1. HPC Laker Profiles
2. ML Historical Essays
3. 2016 GUL Survey
4. "You Know You're from ML if…" Facebook Post (2017-2019)

Bibliography

Correll, Perry W. and Richard W. Koster. 1958. *Picturesque Mountain Lakes*. Mountain Lakes, NJ: Authors.

Crawford, Bruce. "Hippies to Converge on Lakes?" *The Citizen*. 27 August 1970.

Delchamps, Steven. "Street Hockey Hits Mountain Lakes." *The Mountaineer*. March 1973.

Herold, Patricia Reid. 2010. *Mountain Lakes 1911-2011*. Borough of Mountain Lakes, NJ.

Mountain Lakes Historic Preservation Committee. *Historical Essays*. Accessed from *https://mtnlakes.org/about-mountain-lakes/historical-essays/*

Mountain Lakes Historic Preservation Committee. *Laker Profiles*. Accessed from *https://mtnlakes.org/laker-profiles/*

Mountain Lakes Historic Preservation Committee. *National and State Historic District*. Accessed from *https://mtnlakes.org/committees-and-commissions/historic-preservation-committee/national-and-state-historic-district/*

Mountain Lakes High School. *Class Yearbooks* (various years). Accessed from HPC Yearbook Dropbox. *https://www.dropbox.com/sh/vpkub5zeet9m7oi/AADvlmWnP9-7RHlAnrHqXyPra/MLHS%20Yearbooks?dl=0&subfolder_nav_tracking=1*

Mountain Lakes League of Women Voters. (1954, 1967, and 1979). *This is Mountain Lakes*. Mountain Lakes, NJ.

Mueser, Peter. "Lakes Rally Passes Peacefully." *The Citizen*. 27 August 1970.

Obituary of George Wilson. Accessed 1 June 2019 from *https://mackeyfh.com/tribute/details/483/George-Wilson/obituary.html*

Willis, Charles E. 1924. *Scouts of '76: A Tale of the Revolutionary War*. Richmond, VA: Press of the Dietz Printing Co. and Kessinger Legacy Reprints.

www.ingramcontent.com/pod-product-compliance
Lightning Source LLC
Chambersburg PA
CBHW081721100526
44591CB00016B/2458